MAKE YOUTUBE WORK FOR YOUR BUSINESS

The complete guide
to marketing your business,
generating leads, finding
new customers and building
your brand on YouTube.

Alex Stearn

Copyright © 2014 Alex Stearn

All rights reserved.

ISBN-13:978-1502911261
ISBN-10:1502911264

This book is dedicated
to Sonia, Tony and Ollie.

Other Books in the Series

Make Social Media Work For Your Business

Make Facebook Work For Your Business

Make Twitter Work For Your Business

Make Instagram Work For Your Business

Make Pinterest Work For Your Business

Make Google + Work For Your Business

Make Tumblr Work For Your Business

Table of Contents

WHY THIS BOOK?

SO YOU WANT to launch a YouTube marketing campaign for your business or maybe you've already done so and you're just not achieving the results you expected. Perhaps that's because you've found it difficult to build a sizeable following or your audience is simply not converting into paying customers.

Every day hundreds of businesses are setting out on their social media journey excited about the opportunities and possibilities that this relatively new type of marketing may be able to offer their business. Some are getting it right, reaping huge rewards and managing to leverage the enormous power of the internet through YouTube but the majority are struggling to make it work at all. Those who are struggling often don't really understand exactly how to make marketing on YouTube work for their business and launch into a campaign without any plan or strategy or without even knowing exactly what they are looking to achieve. They perhaps create a YouTube account, ask their web developer to add a YouTube button on their website, invite their friends and customers to subscribe and then a start adding their product videos. After a while they realise that whatever they are doing is having little or no positive effect on their sales and they are all left with the same questions:

- How do I leverage the almighty power of the internet and YouTube to make money for my business?

- How do I find the people who are interested in my products?

- How do I draw these people away from YouTube and onto my website or blog?

- And the ultimate question, how do I convert all these people into paying customers and actually profit from YouTube marketing?

These businesses either continue to go round in circles waiting for a miracle to happen, give up altogether or continue to believe that there is a way they can make social media work for their business and start looking for a solution to solve their problem.

This is exactly what I did and this is where my social media journey began. I started to look for a solution but kept coming up with the same brick walls, the same fluffy vague information about engagement and lots of very expensive courses. I read books and blogs but they never really seemed to solve my problem and get to the heart of the matter.

I then decided to make it my mission to demystify the hype surrounding marketing on YouTube and discover everything I possibly could about how to make YouTube and all the other major social media platforms work for any business. I studied literally hundreds of campaigns to see what was working and what wasn't and completely immersed myself in social media marketing until all my questions were answered. My aim was to discover how to utilise the almighty power of YouTube and all the other major social platforms to help any business achieve their marketing goals. I made it my mission to leave no stone unturned in terms of a marketing opportunity which could help any business generate leads and ultimately increase their sales.

After 18 months of immersing myself in this subject I am now delighted to hand this information over to you. My goal is to help you save your time and your resources and provide you with a highly effective system to make YouTube work for your business. In this book I am going to share with you everything you need to know to take your business to the next level, and leverage the power of YouTube marketing, so you can achieve the highest profits, the best customers, the best ambassadors for your business and make money 24/7.

This book is perfect for anyone who is seriously committed to growing their business and achieving incredible results. Whether you are just starting out or already up and running and uncertain how to make YouTube work for your business then this book is to going to teach you exactly how to do just that. You will have absolutely everything you need to learn, prepare, plan and implement a campaign which is going to help you generate leads and find new customers.

The fact is, YouTube and social media as a whole, is a game changer, a dream come true for any business and has completely revolutionised the way business is being done today. However, it is still just a marketing tool and while on the face of it seems free, if not used correctly and effectively it is simply just a waste of your time and resources.

In this book you will not only learn the skills and strategies of YouTube marketing but also everything you need to know about how social media works in marketing and how to plan, prepare and execute your campaign including:

- What social media marketing is, why it is so good, why it is absolutely essential for any business today and why so many businesses are getting it wrong.

- The psychology behind why people make buying decisions and how you can use this knowledge to succeed in your YouTube campaign and on other social platforms as well.

- The importance of defining your business, your brand and your target audience and how to do this.

- How to set clear goals and objectives for your YouTube campaign.

- How to prepare your website or blog for success, capture leads and build a highly targeted list of subscribers.

- How to plan, create, maintain and manage your YouTube campaign.

- Detailed information about how to set up your channel on YouTube.

- The strategies you need to implement to attract the best prospects and build and maintain a targeted following on YouTube and build lasting relationships.

- The importance of content and how to easily find ideas to create content for your target audience.

- How to convert your followers into leads, paying customers and ambassadors and brand advocates of your business.

- How to constantly measure and monitor your campaign so you can steer your campaign to achieve your goals.

A great deal of love has gone into the writing of this book, love of the subject itself and the fact that after researching and devoting 18 months to writing this book and the other books in the series I can finally hand over this information and knowledge to you so you can benefit and profit from my findings. I hope you will be inspired and your business will thrive and flourish as a result of reading and implementing the suggested strategies.

Even within the time it has taken to write this book, certain things have changed in the social media world and so some sections have been updated to reflect those changes. The world of social media is dynamic and therefore it is my commitment to keep updating this book as and when those changes occur. If you wish to keep up to date with latest social media updates, tips and changes please subscribe to my newsletter at www.alexstearn.com

As mentioned above there are books available for each of the major social platforms including, Facebook, Google + Pinterest, Twitter, LinkedIn™, SlideShare, Instagram and Tumblr.

CHAPTER ONE

THE IMPORTANCE OF UNDERSTANDING SOCIAL MEDIA MARKETING

BEFORE LAUNCHING INTO your YouTube marketing campaign and so that you are absolutely committed when you do start you will need to be convinced that social media marketing does actually work for business and that you are going to be able to make it work for yours. In this chapter you will learn why social media marketing has gained so much attention, why so many brands are using it and why it is so different from other forms of marketing. The aim here is to help you to truly appreciate the power and importance of this relatively new method of marketing. Once you are totally convinced that the time you will be investing will be truly worthwhile you will be ready to launch into your YouTube marketing campaign with strength, confidence and conviction.

So what is social media exactly? Social media is the place where people connect with other people using the technology we have today. It's where people engage, share, co-operate, interact, learn, enjoy and build relationships. The number of ways in which we connect with each other has grown massively in recent years from telephone, mobiles, email, text, video, newspaper or radio to what we have today, the social media networks.

As humans the majority of us want to belong, be accepted, loved, respected and heard. We are social animals and social media has provided us with new tools that allow us to be more social even if our lives are more hectic and we are living a long way from our friends and family. It's now not unusual for family and friends to be located at opposite sides of the country or even in a different country. Our lives have become far busier and more transient than ever and yet we still crave the same social connections as we did 100 years ago when we would probably have been living in the same village or town as our family and friends.

The impact that social media is having on our lives and on businesses is massive, social media has completely changed the way we communicate and the way we do everything. It has made connecting with people and building relationships so much easier, now staying in contact with someone we may only have met once is straight forward, we can find old friends we went to school or college with and the opportunities for making new contacts is limitless. Social media has given us the ability to quickly and easily share ideas, experiences and information on anything we like and we can find out about anyone, any business or anything. With the massive growth in smart phone ownership most people can now access the internet instantly, we are living in a virtual world and we can literally connect to anyone, from anywhere, at anytime.

Understanding the reasons why people love social media so much will help give you a really good idea about how, as a business, you need to engage so you can maintain and grow your audience. Most people are on social media to be social, to connect with other family and friends and have fun. However here are a few more reasons why so many use and love social media:

To be part of a community or common interest group.
To express their feelings and have a voice.
To reconnect with old college or school friends.
To find out where their friends are.
To tell their friends where they are.
To find out if a product or service is good.
To connect with thought leaders.
To make business contacts.

To follow brands.

To keep up to date with current affairs, football scores, etc.

To connect with famous people.

To find inspiration and motivation.

To learn by reading blogs, watching videos and listening to podcasts.

To help other people.

To launch a business.

To advertise and grow a business.

To make new friends.

To make new contacts.

To connect with others in different countries.

To make a difference.

To be entertained.

To communicate quickly and save time.

To support important causes or people.

To find a job.

The power and enormity of social media

Everyone is doing Social! Ok, so not everyone is doing social media but the majority of people are! Wherever you go you will see somebody with their heads down looking at some device and you can bet your bottom dollar that they are accessing some social site whether it's YouTube, Twitter, Instagram, LinkedIn, Facebook, Google+, Pinterest or Snapchat.

The growth in social media is huge and it's no wonder that it is being called 'The Social Media Revolution.' Without going into too much statistical information it's safe to say that your customer is probably using at least one social network either for personal or business use and very likely to be accessing multiple sites.

All the social media platforms are growing at incredible speeds and you only have to type 'Social media statistics' into Google and you will blown away by the millions and billions. More than 1 billion unique users visit YouTube per month, Facebook now has over 1 billion users and Twitter has 215 monthly active users. The most popular websites are social. The world loves Social.

What is Social Media Marketing

Not long ago promoting a business could feel very much like being alone on a desert island. You could have a great idea but unless you had vast sums of money for television, magazine or direct mail advertising then frustratingly your idea was very likely to remain a secret. Today it is totally different and social media has given businesses endless opportunities to reach their target audience, connect with new prospects and enter new markets. The playing field has been levelled out and now anyone with the right knowledge has more chance than ever of making their business a success.

Social media marketing is a relatively new form of marketing and refers to the processes, strategies and tactics used by businesses on social networking sites and blogs to gain attention and ultimately increase their revenue. Businesses and large brands are now using the fact that people love to engage and connect with other people with the other very important fact that they are very likely to find their target audience on social media so that they can do the following:

- Find, reach and connect with potential customers.

- Drive traffic to a website or blog.

- Stay connected with, and communicate with, existing customers. It is a well known fact that existing customers are far more likely to purchase and also pay more for a product than someone who has not bought before.

- To build trust, interest and loyalty by interacting with your followers (potential customers) so that ultimately they will purchase your product, continue to purchase your products and hopefully recommend your product to their friends.

- To produce content that users will share with their social network or recommend to their friends. Social media marketing strongly centres around the creation of content for a particular audience with the intention that it can be shared , liked and commented by on the user. When this happens the content is being passed to other users by word of mouth, the most powerful form of advertising.

- To listen and find out what your customers want.

THE BIG LINK, THE PSYCHOLOGY BEHIND BUYING BEHAVIOUR

Not only have successful marketeers recognised that people want to engage with people, they have also tapped into the psychology behind why people make buying decisions and incorporated this into their social media campaigns.

As a business you will need to understand a great deal about your customers in order to market your products successfully to your target audience. Understanding how and why people make the final purchase decision will go a long way in understanding how you can actually make YouTube marketing work for your business. There seem to be a number of factors that influence consumers when they are making their buying decision. Leveraging and using this knowledge with your YouTube campaign is incredibly powerful and a recipe for success.

The Like Factor

This is a Biggie. When we look at the findings and the psychology behind buying decisions it often comes down to simply being likeable. Consumers are far more likely buy a product from someone they like, respect or trust. Word of mouth advertising has always proven to be the most powerful form of advertising and now YouTube has taken this to another level and managed to harness this online with the 'like' and the 'subscribe' button. Having your business name or brand reach hundreds or even thousands of people is now possible and someone only has to 'like' or interact with your business on social media and you can almost guarantee that someone else will see it. The truth is people do business with people they like and are more likely to spread the word to their network about deals and special offers from people they like, trust and respect.

Social proof

When a consumer finds themselves at a point of indecision they will look for social proof and seek advice and corroboration from others. They are far more likely to buy if they see that their friends or a similar group of people have bought or used product. People generally look to others for advice or look to see what others are buying to get over their personal insecurity when making a buying decision. This is why you see so many women shopping in pairs, the opinion of a friend about an item can often be the deciding factor when making the decision to buy or not.

The reason this is so powerful with social media marketing is simply because seeing a large number of people 'liking' a product or service can be enough to persuade someone to make a buying decision, to read something or follow a business. The truth is that people trust the opinion of others more than they trust advertising and in order to make social media marketing work then businesses need to leverage this fact.

Authority and reviews

Even before the internet was introduced people have been keen to find reviews about products they were interested in buying particularly if they were planning to make a major purchase. They would either buy a special magazine or seek information from an authoritative figure on a TV advertisement. Today however shoppers are far more savvy, they can smell an advert a mile off and they will go out of their way to find honest reviews about something they may want to buy. They are also spoilt for choice not only with the number of products available to them but they can find a review about literally anything just by a simple search on the internet or looking at a brand's YouTube channel or their Facebook page. People always have and always will want as much evidence as possible that they are making the right buying decision. Any business who wants to succeed today needs to embrace this fact and try and gain as many reviews for their products and services as possible. Reviews could be in the form of customer blog articles, reviews on your website, on social media sites or articles in newspapers and magazines. Displaying articles, client testimonials or the logos of magazines that you have been featured in on your website will also go a long way to building authority and gaining the trust of your prospects.

Scarcity or exclusivity

Scarcity or exclusivity can play a big part in people buying decisions and YouTube is a perfect place to communicate and use this factor to sell your products. If a product is scarce or less available the consumer will often perceive that this product has greater value and as they become less available the consumer fears that they may lose out on a great deal or a one time offer. Giving your prospects a deadline or a specific time to purchase something or redeem an offer is an incredibly powerful way of focussing their mind to make a decision. When they know they need to make that decision by a certain time or they may lose out on a one time deal they are far more likely to make that decision. Another very effective way of using this factor is by simply suggesting to your prospects that by signing up for your email opt-in, they will be the first to see your next video or to hear about your new products, or your exclusive offers.

Consistency

Consumers do not like taking risks and often prefer to repeat their past purchasing behaviour by buying from a brand they have bought from before. The majority of shoppers are brand loyal and social media is another way of nurturing this type of behaviour by building up even deeper relationships with your customers through constant contact and updates.

Reciprocation

Reciprocation is a very powerful factor to take into consideration if you are looking to succeed on YouTube. As humans, the majority of us have a natural desire to repay favours and with YouTube you can really put this into practise. If you show support by either liking, subscribing, sharing or commenting on other peoples video content not only will it attract their attention they will, more often than not, return the favour by 'liking,' commenting, subscribing and sharing your content. Also if you are sharing great content on your network or offering good, valuable and free advice you are very likely to earn a great deal of respect and this will often result in a good pay back of some sort.

WHY IS SOCIAL MEDIA MARKETING SO GOOD FOR YOUR BUSINESS?

We know that an enormous number of people are accessing the social networks to connect with each other and now we need to understand why this type of marketing is so different from other forms of marketing and why it is so important for your business. The main reason is that social media marketing is fundamentally more effective. Consumers today are smart, they are tired and suspicious of traditional forms of advertising, more often than not they will fast forward a TV commercial, switch channel or skip a printed page with an advertisement on it. Todays consumers want to hear that a product has been tried and tested, they want to see a product being demonstrated and they often need a recommendation from a trusted source to make a purchase, most probably a friend. Here are some reasons why social media marketing is more effective than other more traditional marketing methods:

Social media offers you the opportunity to find the right target audience

Never before has it been so easy to find and access your target audience. With the information that YouTube and most of the social networks hold about their users you can now target and find the very people who are more likely to buy your products or services.

Social media allows you to have a direct contact with your customer
Literally you have the opportunity to communicate directly and stay in touch with your customer, unlike traditional forms of advertising. If you manage to get a user to subscribe to your channel or sign up to you opt-in then you can stay in touch and continue to build your relationship.

Social media marketing harnesses the power of peer recommendation

The majority of people trust recommendations by others. Social media marketing is the only media that can harness the most powerful form of advertising, word of mouth, by making it possible for consumers to communicate with each other and vote for products or services by pressing the 'like' or 'subscribe' button.

Helps builds your brand
Never has there been so much opportunity to build your brand. Your brand is simply your most valuable asset of your business. Your brand is what differentiates you from other businesses, it is the image people have of your business and it establishes loyalty. With social media you have the opportunity to engage with consumers and build positive brand associations in a way that no other media can. Consumers now have the choice and opportunity to follow your brand and if they do, this means they actually want to hear or see what you have to say.

Humanises your brand
Social media allows you to communicate with your audience in a totally unique way. Your brand is no longer a rigid logo but a personality, not only can you show your appreciation and the value you place on your audience but they can also grow to love your brand too. No other type of

marketing allows this type of two way live communication.

Offers continual exposure to your product

Social media marketing allows you to be continually in contact with your followers. Once you have your audience they can hear from you and see your brand on a daily basis. Statistics prove that on average a person needs to see or connect with a brand 7 times before they buying it. This is a difficult and costly goal to achieve with traditional forms of advertising but incredibly easy with social media marketing.

The Consumer has a choice

Unlike other traditional methods of advertising the consumer has the opportunity to be exposed to your product by choice, they can opt in or out whenever they want.

Your audience is relaxed and receptive

The majority of people are accessing their social networks in their own leisure time. People are far more receptive to hearing from a brand in their own time when they are relaxed, as long as the brand is not continually pushing their product.

You can continually engage with your audience

Social media marketing allows you to have an ongoing dialogue with your audience like no other media. Fans or followers who have interacted with a business on social media are far more likely to visit their online store than those who did not.

It's viral

Once your followers choose to interact or share your content then this interaction is seen by their network of friends who are then also exposed to your brand. This is how viral growth happens which results in audience growth and brand awareness, more prospects, more customers and increased sales.

Social media is an asset to your business

Unlike other forms of advertising where you see your marketing investment disappear your YouTube channel or any other social account becomes a valuable asset. If you are using your social media marketing correctly your network will grow, you will be building trust and your asset will increase in value. With traditional advertising once an advert is delivered the connection with the buyer is over and you see your investment literally disappear.

It is like having your own broadcasting channel

Once you have your campaign set up and your follower numbers are growing, you literally have your very own broadcasting channel which you own. You can communicate with your followers about anything 24/7. Nobody can take this away unless of course you are not running it correctly and you are losing subscribers. If you provide content that is so useful and interesting, your subscribers will keep coming back again and again to check if you have anything new to say. You then have a following of people who will associate your valuable content and their positive experience with your brand.

You can offer your customers proof of trading

Having a social media presence which is active and engaging helps to reassure customers that your business actually exists. They can easily check, by comments left by customers, whether your business is reputable and trustworthy and they are far more likely to buy from you once they see your active presence on social media.

Improve your search engine ranking

Google counts social sharing when ranking your website or blog. If people are finding your content valuable then the search engines will register that and then rank you accordingly. Social media sites are highly ranked in the search engines and having a well optimised profile is yet another way of being found on the internet. YouTube videos are very highly ranked.

Opens up a worldwide playing field

It used to be only the large companies who could afford to build their brand and have the opportunity to access thousands of potential customers. Now everybody with a business has the opportunity to reach thousands of people both nationally and globally, grow their business and benefit from one of the most powerful forms of marketing. Having a business no longer has to be a lonely island you literally have the opportunity to get your message heard by thousands of people through social networking.

Provides advantages for the consumer

With just a few clicks of the mouse or the tap of a smart phone, consumers can be in contact with any business very quickly. For once their opinions are important, taken seriously and valued, they can contact a brand for customer service issues or just follow a brand because they are interested. For the first time they have a voice and a very powerful one. This is showing in the continual rise in the number of people following brands. People want to remain close to the brands they are interested in.

You can listen to your customers

You can now hear what your customers are saying about your product or service and you can use this information to improve or develop your products and improve your customer service. This will result in your business becoming more transparent and shows your customers that you care and value their opinion which ultimately leads to more trust for your brand.

You can become a thought leader

By producing valuable and rich content for your audience you can become a thought leader. Not only will this help if you are a personal brand but will also help in building respect and reputation for any business or brand.

You can make a difference

With social media you can actually make a positive difference to people's lives. Once you know your audience you can provide content for them which is of value to them and is actually going to help them in some way. Helping your audience like this goes a long way and will hopefully result in them remembering your business when they are ready to make that purchasing decision.

Endless opportunities

Never has there been so much opportunity to have direct access to so many people and neither has there been so much opportunity for businesses of any size to have ongoing contact with so many of their potential customers. This is a marketeer or business owner's dream.

IS SOCIAL MEDIA ACTUALLY WORKING FOR BUSINESS?

It is evident that the majority of major brands are running successful social media marketing campaigns. These brands are investing huge amounts of money, time and resources into this type of marketing, however you don't have to go too far to see whether social media marketing is actually working for business, simply ask yourself these questions:

- Would you prefer to buy a product if you knew that a friend or somebody you know of had tried it?

- Would you prefer to buy a product from a business or person that you do know rather than a business or person that you don't know?

- If you were thinking of buying a product from a business you had no history with, would you go and look to see if they had a social media site and see what other people were saying about their product?

If you answered yes to these questions then you can be pretty sure that social media marketing does actually work for businesses. It has to work doesn't it?

WHY SO MANY BUSINESSES ARE GETTING IT WRONG

Even though most business owners have heard how powerful social media marketing can be the majority are still unsure as to how to use it to benefit their business. So many YouTube channels have been created with enthusiasm only to be abandoned a couple of months even weeks down the line. Others are painstakingly uploading video content regularly but uploading the wrong type of content without a clue how to get their fans to buy their products. Many businesses are just paying lip service and seem to think that displaying a few social media icons on their site is enough to miraculously increase their revenue and some are not even connected to any networks at all. Although on the face of it, social media marketing seems free it actually takes a sizeable investment of man hours, and if you are getting it wrong you may as well be throwing a great deal of money out of the window. Here are some common reasons why so many businesses are getting it wrong:

Not 100% committed and convinced

Many businesses are not convinced that it actually works at all and therefore are not prepared to put in the time it takes to learn how to plan and implement the effective strategies it takes to build a successful campaign. As a result their campaign falls flat and they simply give up after a few months.

Little or no understanding about how social media marketing works

Many still think that setting up an account and putting an icon on their website is what it's all about. They may even upload a few product videos in the hope that their website is suddenly going to be inundated with new traffic and think that these new visitors are miraculously going to convert into customers.

They don't understand the fact that subscribers, fans and followers are worthless unless they know what to do with them

Just because a business has maybe 1000 or 30,000 subscribers, fans or followers, does not mean this will automatically transfer to their balance sheet. Subscribers are just subscribers, and as long a business doesn't know what do with those subscribers they will stay as just subscribers and not customers.

Not understanding the psychology behind buying decisions

They have absolutely no idea about the psychology behind how and why people make buying decisions and therefore, do not know how to use this knowledge to their advantage in their campaign.

Lack of clear goals

Aimlessly sharing content on their network without setting specific and measurable goals is just a waste of time and resources.

Not having a system to capture and convert leads

Building a following is almost useless if those followers are not visiting the business' website or subscribing to the newsletter so that they can be converted into paying customers. Many businesses are still not making lead capture one of their main goals.

Unrealistic expectations

Social media is a long terms strategy, it needs to be an integral part of a business' marketing plan and today it's as important as any other daily task a business may undertake. It is not a one size fits all solution and is not a solution for overnight success. It takes careful planning and long term commitment.

The wrong audience

It's no good having a huge number of followers if they are not the correct audience. There are even sites where you can buy followers, but if they are not the right audience then they are very unlikely to be interested in what that business has to offer.

Not enough followers

The majority of businesses are going to need a sizeable audience to make any impact at all, and although engagement is important, unless a business has a healthy number of followers it's not going to be a great deal of benefit.

Not being proactive

Many businesses seem to assume that people are just going to press the 'subscribe,' 'like' or 'follow' or button on their blog or website. Unfortunately it doesn't work like that and people generally need a good reason or incentive to follow a business, unless it's a very well known brand.

Trying to push their products all the time

This is not what social media marketing is about and businesses that continually push their products are just missing the whole point of how social media marketing works and will lose followers as a result.

Posting too little, posting too often, or posting the wrong content altogether

If you post too much your posts will be considered as spam. If you post too little you will just be forgotten and if you post the wrong content you will not attract the right audience which may harm your brand. In an online survey top three reasons for losing followers were:

i.) The Company posted too frequently

ii.) The business pushed their products too much

iii.) The business posted offensive content

Chapter Two

How to Run a Successful YouTube Marketing Campaign, an Overview

ONCE YOU HAVE made the decision to be 100% committed to your campaign, you fully understand the theory behind it and you plan and implement the strategies and tactics outlined in this book your business is going to reap the benefits and you will in time develop an extremely valuable asset. One thing is for certain if you choose to ignore social media you can be sure that your competition will not and you'll be allowing them to steal the advantage. Social media is a powerful way to increase your revenue by driving sales, increasing customer loyalty and building your brand while at the same time pushing down your cost of sales, marketing, customer service and much more. Now let's get started!

So how do you leverage the power of social media and put it to work to benefit your business and produce amazing results? This chapter is designed to give you a brief overview about what is required to build a successful campaign so that as and when you read each chapter it will make more sense. Every aspect of this overview and everything you need to do and implement will be mapped out clearly for you in the subsequent chapters.

The opportunity to reach an unlimited number of new contacts and prospects is available to every business today. You can safely say that your prospects are out there and all you need to do is know where to find them, how to connect with them and then how to capture and convert them into your customers.

Successful businesses are using YouTube and the other social media platforms in a totally different way to that of traditional methods of marketing. With YouTube marketing there is no need to employ pushy sales techniques. Once you put the essential work, planning and system in place you will find your products are practically selling themselves and your prospects are buying your products and becoming your brand advocates as a natural progression from your initial contact with them. The whole process is straight forward and as long as you carry out the necessary background work, planning and preparation you can make it work for your business.

Know what you want

You need to have a good idea about where you want your business to go in the next 1−3 years, if you don't know what you want then it is unlikely that your business will achieve anywhere near its potential. When you have a clear vision for your business it helps you to focus and create the necessary goals you need to put into place to achieve that vision.

Define your business and your brand and your target audience

Brands establish customer loyalty and YouTube offers you a huge opportunity to build your brand. In order to communicate in the right way you need to create and consistently deliver the right message and brand experience to your prospects and customers. To do this you need to define your business and define and understand your target audience so you can create your brand.

Plan, plan, plan

Social media is not a quick fix, the majority of businesses start a campaign and then fall by the wayside. If you want to grow your business then careful planning is required which involves: creating your mission statement, setting clear and measurable goals and objectives, planning your system for lead capture and planning your content strategy in line with who and what your target audience want. Putting a good plan and system into place will take all the guess work, worry and stress out of your campaign and give you confidence and direction. You will find that the campaign will be almost running itself and working like a machine producing leads and customers. Without a carefully crafted plan your campaign is extremely unlikely to succeed and you will waste huge amounts of time and resources.

Prepare your business

Before launching your campaign you need to prepare your whole business so your brand and your brand message is evident throughout. You will need to communicate your brand through everything your do or say including all your marketing material, brochures, promotional material, your website, your blog and your email.

Your website is one of the best sales people you can have, it works 24/7 and can turn up in your customer's home at the click of a mouse. When your prospect arrives on your website you need to make them feel they have arrived at the right place and that you understand their needs and can either provide a solution or give them exactly what they want. If you already have a website then you need to check it has all the necessary features it takes to grab your visitors attention, deliver the right message, capture them and convert them into customers. Statistics prove that unless a business has a clever method of capturing leads then the majority of visitors to a website will leave without buying anything or ever returning again. Therefore before even starting your YouTube campaign you will need to check or create your website so that it does the job it is supposed to which is to capture leads and convert them into customers.

Set up your email campaign

Email is still one of the most effective methods of converting leads and therefore you will need to set up an account with an email service provider and plan your email campaign so you can continue to build a relationship with your prospect, build trust and sell your products.

Create your YouTube Channel

Your YouTube channel will in many cases be the first impression your prospects have about your business and is as important as your website or blog. The aim of your channel is to capture your prospects by getting to subscribe to your channel so that you can continue to communicate and build a relationship with them through though uploading new videos and by getting them to join your opt-in. You will need to create your YouTube trailer video which is an introduction to your channel, complete all the necessary descriptions and information for your channel.

Create your YouTube Video Content calendar

Social media is not like traditional forms of advertising so frequently pushing your products, posting adverts and plugging your business is not going to work and is likely to lose you subscribers. One of the most important things you are going to have to do for a successful YouTube campaign is to regularly produce and upload compelling content that your audience actually wants to engage with and share. YouTube marketing is all about selling without selling and the aim of producing content is not to directly sell your products but to do the following:

- Boost traffic to your blog or website, generate, capture and nurture leads.
- Create brand awareness.
- Create a personal connection with your audience through video.
- Constantly remind your audience of your brand so when they are ready to buy they buy from you.
- Improve your ranking in the search engines.
- Create engagement, build relationships and encourage your audience to share your content with their friends.
- Support others by liking, commenting on and sharing their content.
- Stand out as a thought leader and build your reputation as an expert in your industry.

- Create such good content that your audience stays liking your page and continuing to read your updates which builds and encourage brand loyalty.

Your content is where you can connect with your audience through their interests and passions. Your quality of content needs to be outstanding and you need to delight your audience with the best possible fresh, new and compelling material, excellence is what you should be aiming for every time you post. The biggest thing to remember is that you need to tailor all your content to your audience's desires and needs.

Once you are absolutely clear about who your target audience is, what makes them tick, and what their values and aspirations are you can determine what subjects and topics they will be interested in. The majority of the content you post will need to be about their needs and not yours. There is nothing more off putting and likely to lose you followers than continually posting about your business and shouting about your products or services. Of course you can do this occasionally if you have new products or special offers but you need to be selective otherwise your posts just become bad noise. Remember your followers are mostly on YouTube to be entertained and if your posts ruin their experience they will associate your brand with a bad experience and it won't be long before you start losing your subscribers and potential customers.

When you have decided on the subjects and topics you are going to create content about, then you will need to create a YouTube content calendar which will help you to consistently deliver this high quality content. You will need to incorporate everything in this calendar including any events you are planning, any special industry events, public holidays, blog posts, videos and offers or contests you may be planning. You then need to map it all out so you know exactly how you are going to promote them on YouTube with the functionality you have available to do so.

Build a sizeable and highly targeted following

The main aim of building your audience is to grow a community of followers who are interested in your products, will engage with your content and become advocates for your brand. In order to have any impact at all you are going to need a sizeable number of targeted followers on YouTube. Building your audience is going to be an ongoing task and involve many different strategies all covered in this book. The size and time it takes to build your audience will depend on the time and resources you have available. However, do not get overwhelmed and compare yourself with those who have got thousands of subscribers, it's more important to concentrate your efforts on targeting the right audience and then delighting them with great content. This way you will benefit from everything that goes with a highly engaged audience by delivering a great brand experience and you will find your audience naturally growing in a very positive way.

The essential day to day activity

To build a strong presence, build trust, build relationships and reputation you will need to be active and nurture your subscribers. Social media is not a one way street, it's an ongoing two way communication, it's about going out and showing that you are interested in what others have to say and it's about building community and getting your brand out there in the most positive light possible. Here are some of the things you will need to do on a day to day basis:

- Consistently post high quality content.

- Follow your subscribers.

- Engage, comment, share and reply.

- Show your audience you value and respect them.

- Follow influencers in your niche.

- Deal with negative comments.

Analysing and measuring your campaign results

This book is all about how to make YouTube work for your business and the only way you are going to find out if it is working or not is by constantly monitoring and analysing your results. You will need to constantly check your results against the goals and objectives you have set. Once you know what is working and what is not then you can adjust and steer your campaign accordingly, to achieve more positive results.

CHAPTER THREE

GETTING STARTED ON YOUTUBE

YOUTUBE IS NOT only the worlds largest video sharing site and the second largest search engine, it is also a social network, a vibrant community of people who want to learn, be entertained, interact with each other and share content, and an advertising platform. The growth in the number of people with smart phones, together with increased availability and speed of the internet has fuelled an explosion in the number of videos viewed. YouTube is now seeing over four billion video views per day with over one billion unique users per month. These people are not necessarily going to YouTube to buy products and services, but they are going there to watch videos, be entertained, to find out about things they are interested in, or to find out how to do things. Any business that understands this and can produce interesting and compelling content aimed at the interests of their target audience has the opportunity to reap the marketing benefits that YouTube has to offer.

However, even though YouTube is the second largest search engine, many businesses are still ignoring it as a serious platform for finding new customers and building their brand. The fact is video and YouTube offer huge potential for businesses to generate leads, gain exposure and build their brand, particularly since businesses are far more likely to get video content ranked in Google search than any text article.

The main reasons why many businesses are frightened off, is because they think it's either too complicated, too expensive, too time consuming or they fear standing in front of a camera. But the truth is, producing videos no longer needs to be expensive or time consuming. Investing in high quality camera equipment is not always necessary and with today's smart phone technology creating quality videos is now relatively easy and inexpensive. Many of the most popular viral videos have been created on a phone or webcam. With regard to editing and production the availability of applications like 'iMovie' and 'Final Cut' have made uploading and editing videos incredibly straight forward and now YouTube has free editing features as well. Videos can now be easily embedded into websites, blogs and other social media with little or no technical expertise.

The very fact that YouTube is being under utilised by so many businesses means there is huge potential for those businesses who want to use it properly. Before you make any decision about whether YouTube is a viable platform to market your business, here are some reasons why deciding to use video and YouTube may be one of the smartest decisions you make:

A powerful platform to generate leads for your business
This has got to be the most important benefit for any business. As the second largest search engine YouTube is a very powerful platform for generating leads and driving traffic to a website by helping consumers find answers to their questions and search queries. Any business that realises the huge potential available on YouTube to find new customers and then puts in a system to capture leads and convert them into paying customers is going to be onto a winner.

Fact, video sells stuff!
It just does. Viewers are three times more likely to purchase an item after watching a video.

Video levels the playing field
Video lets you compete with large companies and allows you to reach and communicate with your audience relatively inexpensively.

Creates a deeper relationship with your audience

People like to connect with people and face to face video content can create the deepest possible connection with any audience. If you or one of your colleagues become the face of your brand the relationship with your target audience will become much deeper, more powerful and more lasting. Video also creates a lasting impression and is well remembered which is powerful for any brand.

Video is mobile

With the increase in mobile devices businesses have even more opportunity to communicate with their target audience. Since people carry their mobiles on them most of time it is even more likely that a video will be viewed, as consumers can choose to watch in their own time and at their leisure. They are often more receptive, because if they do watch a video it's because they actually want to and not because they are forced too. People will also often read their mail on their phone in their leisure time so any video attached to that mail is also more likely to get watched, than if they are at their desk.

People love video

YouTube videos are appearing very high in search engine results and also consumers are going straight to YouTube with their questions, they are looking for businesses like yours to answer those questions in the most concise and straight forward way, which is often by video. Videos can deliver information in the most easy to understand form and videos can inspire, educate and entertain all at the same time. Most people would much rather watch a video than read a lengthy time consuming and complex instructional document, also 90% of information transmitted to the brain is visual and processed faster in the brain than text. According to a study performed by Forbes in association with Google, 75% of business executives watch a work-related video weekly and more than half of them watch a video on YouTube.

Drives traffic to websites

Videos drive traffic to websites. In the same study, Forbes discovered that 65% of executives visited a vendor's website after viewing a video and the younger executives particularly were more engaged and likely to make a purchase or call the vendor and share the video with other colleagues.

Increases sales conversions

Having a video on your site is like having a sales person active 24/7 and website visitors are more likely to buy a product on an online retail site after watching a video. Viewers spend more time on pages with videos and increase click through rates too.

Increases your email open rates

Videos increase email open rates and can decrease the number of opt-outs from your subscribers. The fact is, a good proportion of people would much rather watch a quick video than read an email and people like to connect with people.

Powerful for building your personal brand

There is no better way of creating a personal connection and building trust with your audience than with video. If you are your own personal brand then video is almost essential. It is incredibly powerful and offers you the opportunity to reach people in locations that you would never have had the opportunity of reaching before. If you produce good video, then you will be streets ahead of anyone who is just creating a blog and video will definitely give you the edge. There are numerous types of video you can use to help all areas of your business including regular Vlogs, instructional videos, coaching sessions and Webinars, you can also utilise Google 'Hangouts on Air'.

Videos get shared

YouTube videos are the number one type of content to get shared on social media, 700 videos a minute are shared on Twitter alone! Visual content also drives engagement which means it gets liked and commented on and therefore can help you to grow your reach and amplify your message.

Powerful for search engine optimisation

YouTube is owned by Google and therefore YouTube videos get highly ranked within Google. Recent statistics show that a video is far more likely to get ranked in Google than a text page and far more likely to get viewed than any blog post. YouTube thumbnails often appear in Google search results which also increases click through and videos also help with your SEO by attracting more back links than plain text posts.

Makes your business stand out

Videos are almost always unique in their creation and are a great way to make your mark and stand out from the crowd. Consumers are far more likely to purchase from someone they have built a relationship with and video is the best way to deliver your message personally to a large number of people.

Video is continually working for you

Once your video is on the internet it can be continually working for you and it's like having a sales team working 24/7 for you which makes it an incredibly inexpensive method of promotion.

HOW YOUTUBE CAN BENEFIT YOUR BUSINESS

Quite simply YouTube means traffic, leads and sales. People love to watch video for all sorts of reasons and video executed properly can create the deepest possible connection with any audience and more than any other type of media.

There are four possible ways that you can make money through YouTube and these are:

- By creating video content to promote your own business and your own products by using YouTube as a traffic source, improving your search engine optimisation, generating leads and building your brand.

• Making money from advertising on your videos with Google's Adsense.

• Affiliate marketing.

• Sponsorship.

The aim of this book is to outline how you can use YouTube as a traffic source, how to create compelling video content and outline the strategies and tactics you will need to implement to generate and capture leads, increase your sales and build your brand.

In order to make YouTube work for your business you will need to define and create clear goals, objectives and strategies. Here are some goals that you may wish to achieve for your business through using YouTube:

To use YouTube as a traffic and lead generator
To find new customers by creating compelling content, capturing leads and converting them into new customers with the use of your opt in list or by creating a sales funnel.
Example objectives:
• To create X Number of new leads per day.
• To add X number of new subscribers to email opt in
• To create X number of sales through sales funnel each day.

To inform your customers
Keep existing customers interested in products and keep them talking about and sharing your content.
Example objective: To create 1 Video per week/month

To become a thought leader in your industry and build your brand
Example Objective: To create consistently create video and at least 1 new video per week on a new subject relating to the industry.

To build a loyal following of subscribers and a community
Example Objective: To have X number of subscribers on channel in 1/6/12 months

To support your PR by adding a video with your PR releases
Example Objective: To add a video to every press release that is sent out.

To improve your sites search engine optimisation through adding video to your site
It is thought that you should have self hosted videos on your site for selling your products, but this does not stop you from uploading them to YouTube as well and you may make some sales from your YouTube channel.
Example Objective: To add 1 Video demonstrating each product on website.

To enhance your blog posts with video
Example objective: To produce a video for every blog post to encourage more traffic from YouTube and to support the blog with video content as well to increase reach through YouTube.

To support your social media goals
Example objective: To support your social media goals by providing video content for your other social media platforms.

To capture leads from other channels to convert to sales
Example Objective: To create X number of videos per week/month to share on other social media platforms.

To support your PPC Advertising by remarketing

With ads on YouTube and across the Google display network you can remarket and advertise to people who have already watched any of your YouTube videos or subscribed or unsubscibed to your channel.

FINDING YOUR WAY AROUND YOUTUBE

Once you have created your account on YouTube it's a really good idea to have a look around and familiarise yourself with your account and your channel. Once you get to know YouTube you will find just how much it has to offer and just how straightforward it is to use. This section will give you a quick introduction to finding your way around YouTube and an explanation of the terms which will be mentioned throughout this book. If you are new to YouTube then this section will be really helpful.

By clicking on your channel icon on the top right of your screen you will display the following : My Channel, Video Manager, Subscriptions, Settings, Switch Account and Sign out.

My Channel

Home. When you click on 'My channel' you will arrive on your channel home page where you will be able to view your channel art with your channel icon and links to your website and social platforms, if you have added them.

Underneath your channel art you will be able to upload your trailer video. This video will be displayed alongside a description which is taken from the video description. You need to make this your welcome message. Your channel trailer is available if you have your 'Channel browse view' enabled. To enable, simply click on the pencil icon and then click on 'Edit channel navigation' and then click on 'Enable' in the 'Browse section' The 'Browse' view of your channel allows visitors to see the customised content (the channel trailer sections) you are displaying. Disabling the 'Browse' view will display your channel feed to all users.

Under your trailer video your viewers will be able to view the videos you have uploaded. You can organise your videos into sections. Sections let you feature sets of videos, such as your latest uploads or likes, or you can feature a custom set by using a playlist or tag. You can display your sections either as a horizontal row or a vertical list.

On the right you will see 'Popular channels' which have been selected by YouTube and also 'Featured Channels' which are the favourite channels you have chosen to display. You can choose to disable your 'Popular channels' but in doing so you will stop your channel from being recommended across YouTube on other channels.

You can see how the public view your channel by clicking 'View as public' on the top right of you channel art.

Videos
Your videos page shows all the videos you have uploaded in chronological order and also displays other videos that you have liked. You can choose whether you want to display the videos you have liked to the public or not.

Playlists
Playlists make it possible for your viewers to watch multiple videos with minimal effort. Playlists are proven to increase view time and they also appear in search results and suggested videos so it is a very good idea to create them. You can create your own playlists and organise your videos into different sets or groups that relate to each other in some way. When you create your playlist you need to add a title and create a description for your playlist, this is your metadata which YouTube uses to index your videos and therefore you need to optimise your title, description and tags with specific keywords from your niche which also relate to your content. In your description you can include links to subscribe to your channel and other related videos and playlists.

You can use playlist to do the following:

- To group videos together that you want your viewers to watch in one session.
- To group videos around a subject or theme.
- To combine your most popular content for your more recent uploads.
- To group your most viewed videos to tempt your viewer to watch your best content.

Discussions

Discussions are where your viewers can leave comments about your channel and you can reply to them. This is a real opportunity to build relationships. If people are leaving positive comments then they are interested and it's only courteous to thank them and reply.

About

Your about section is where you add your channel description, your links and add your featured channels. It is also where you can display the channel which you are subscribed to and you can make this public or not.

The Dashboard

The dashboard is like the back office of your YouTube account and it is here you can find all the following, Video Manager, Community, Channel settings, Analytics and Creation Tools. You find your dashboard by clicking on the gear icon on the top right.

Video Manager

Your video manager is just that, it is where you upload and manage your videos and you will find the following:

- **Uploads** This is where you upload and edit your videos, add annotations, enhancements, add audio, add captions and add all your descriptions, titles and tags. You can also add your videos to playlists here.

- **Live Events** You can stream live events on YouTube. To do this you will need to go to 'Channel Settings' and enable 'live events'. If your account is in good order and you have more than 100 subscriber you will able to stream live events. With the right planning, testing and promotion you can use this functionality to broadcast live events like news, cultural or music events. There are full instruction on YouTube how to do this. You can also create 'Hangouts on Air' which encourage subscriber engagement and require less technical knowledge. More about Hangouts on Air later.

- **Playlists** This shows all your play lists.

- **Tags** This shows all the tags you have used.

- **Search history** Your search history is really useful and lets you see what you have previously searched for on YouTube which may help you find a particular video.

- **Favourites** This shows all the videos that you have favourited. To favourite a video simply click 'Add to' under the video you are watching and then you can choose where you want to add it to, either a playlist or your favourites.

- **Likes** This show all the videos you have liked.

Community
Community is where you can manage your comment settings and where you can manage your inbox.

Channel Settings

- **Features** This tells you how your account stands and what your account has been enabled to do, for example, whether your account has been enabled for monetization, longer videos , live events and whether you can upload custom thumbnails.

- **Defaults** This is where you can set your defaults for future video uploads. You can override these settings on individual videos.

- **In video Programming** This is a feature that lets you embed a chosen video or logo across all of your videos on your channel. By adding your channel avatar as an annotation you can lead viewers to your channel page and by adding a thumbnail annotation you can lead viewers to the video watch page.

- **Fan Finder** Fan finder helps to find and connect your channel to new fans at no cost to you . YouTube uses the information they have about what their viewers are watching and tries to match your channel with people they think may enjoy your videos. When you create your channel advert make sure it is as short and engaging as possible, after five seconds your viewer can skip, so your aim here is to make it so engaging that they do not do that. Make sure you show your viewers what your channel is about, make it clear why they should subscribe to your channel and include a call to action and an annotation.

- **Advanced** This is where you can choose whether or not you want to allow adverts to be displayed, where you can link your Adwords account and add an associated website URL . You can also specify here whether you want to display the number of subscribers you have and also if you want your channel to appear in other channels' recommendations.

Analytics

Analytics lets you measure and analyse your organic and paid traffic and view all your reports. This is explained in more detail in the chapter about measuring your campaign results.

Creation Tools

- **Audio Library** This is where you can download royalty free audio for your videos.

- Video Editor This is where you can edit your videos and add images, audio, transitions and titles.

SETTING UP YOUR SYSTEM TO GENERATE AND CAPTURE LEADS

Before we go into how you are going to get tons of subscribers and traffic to your channel you will need to have a system in place so that you can capture leads and convert them into sales. Without some kind of strategy you are just wasting time and money. Inspiring videos are great to build your brand and stand out from the crowd but in order to let them really work for your business they need to help you to generate and capture leads so you can convert them into paying customers.

The one time that most people are going to be interested in you is when they have found and watched your video. This is when they need your information, they may not be ready to buy your product yet but this is when they are most likely to subscribe and opt into your list.

Basically your videos are your tool to generate and capture new leads and channel then into your sales funnel. You simply create compelling video content that your audience will love with the sole intention of getting them onto your list by offering them something of value for free. Once they are on your list you have the opportunity to convert these leads into customers.

Here is a quick step by step process showing how to do it:

1. Create your special free offer

Firstly you need to think of something that your target audience really want and it needs to be something they would consider really valuable, this could be a free ebook, a short video course or a Webinar about a really hot topic or a special money offer coupon. Webinars and videos can be incredibly effective as they help to create an immediate personal connection with your audience from the start which can be extremely powerful as people generally like to buy from people they like and trust. When choosing your offer you need to ask yourself this one question: is this valuable enough that it is my ideal customer would pay for it? If your answer to this question is yes, then this is probably the right offer and you are likely to persuade them to volunteer their email. If your answer is no then you will need to think again. This really is one of the most important parts of this lead generation system and in order to create a really positive first experience with your prospect you need to really wow them with your offer.

2. Create your landing page

You will then need to create a special landing page with your offer and your email opt-in capture form. You can either ask a web developer to create this for you or use a landing page generator service like, www.leadpages.com , www.launcheffect.com or www.instapage.com or www.unbounce.com . For a monthly fee these websites offer an incredibly user friendly service with numerous templates, design examples and tutorials to help you put your landing page together. Your landing page needs to be specific to the one goal you want to achieve which is to visually promote your offer and then capture the email addresses of your prospects. Make sure you set up your opt-in email list with your email service provider first. Providers include www.aweber.com www.constantcontact.com or www.mailchimp.com

3. Create your video

Create a video which is aimed at the interests of your target audience.

4. Include a call to action and send them to your landing page

Include a strong call to action at the end of the video to sign up for a free offer, making sure you give the viewer enough time to take that action

5. Send them to a thank you page

By this time you will have their email and you will need to:

- Thank them for purchasing.
- Deliver the free gift.
- Offer them another gift or bonus gift for sharing you on other social networks.

CHAPTER FOUR

CONTENT IS KING ON YOUTUBE

WHETHER YOU ARE creating your own videos or employing a production company you will need to create consistently exceptional video content which is going to be of value to your target audience. There are definitely certain factors that will enhance your viewers experience and contribute to making your videos a success, but the most important elements are your subject and its content.

When it comes to your content simply standing in front of a camera advertising your product is not going to work. You will need to produce content that is going to either interest, entertain or help your audience in some way. This is not saying you should not produce the occasional product video, but in order to win new viewers and build an audience you will need to get creative and produce compelling content around subjects that your audience are searching for. By offering this information you will have more chance of capturing the right audience through YouTube and Google and converting them into customers by building a relationship and trust with your audience.

To start you need to research your target audience, find out who they are and what they are interested in and what they want. Once you have this information you can think about the sort of content that you can create around these subjects. Google's Keyword Planner is a very effective way of finding out what particular keywords people are searching for around your products or services. The Keyword Planner will also help by offering you information on the average number of times a word is searched for and the amount of competition for that word. You can even view a graph which displays seasonal trends to help you to decide when the best time is to promote your video in order to receive the maximum possible number of views.

IDEAS FOR DIFFERENT TYPES OF VIDEO CONTENT

Once you are clear about your subject or topic you can decide which type of video you want to create. Here are some ideas for the different types of video that you can create on YouTube.

Your YouTube trailer video

The first video you need to create is you Your Tube trailer video. Your channel trailer is the introduction video to your channel and is the first video that your unsubscribed visitors will see when they view your channel. Before creating this video you need to ask yourself these questions:

What do my audience really want to hear?
What value can I offer my subscribers?
How can I best convince first time unsubscribed visitors to subscribe to my channel?
How can I make this compelling enough and interesting enough?
How can I deliver this in the most unique way?

Make sure when creating it you keep it short and straight to the point, describe your channel, add a call to action and at the end of the video ask viewers to subscribe. Do make sure the viewer has time to take action before the video finishes. Clicking the edit pencil lets you add or remove or trailer

Video blogging

Vlogging or video blogging is a form of blogging using video. Video blogging opens up a whole new world to smaller businesses who otherwise would not be able to afford the high cost of television advertising. If you are a personal brand then vlogging can be a very effective way of creating a successful channel on YouTube and building your brand.

By putting a face to your business you instantly create a connection with your audience like no other media and is even better because your audience can actually interact with you and your content by writing comments, asking questions and sharing your content.

Video Blogging is the single most powerful and inexpensive way to build a lasting connection and relationship with your audience. Delivering content on a regular basis helps to draw attention to your brand, promotes interaction and helps to build trust with your audience. It keeps your current customers interested and engaged and gives potential customers a fast introduction to what your business is all about. Vlogging also helps to make you stand out as an authority on your subject, so when it comes to your prospects making a purchasing decision, they will be more likely to buy from you.

How you produce your videos will depend very much on your budget, you can either produce your own videos with very little expense using a webcam, iphone or video camera, or you can employ a production company to produce them. If you do decide to use a production company then most companies will be willing to produce videos for you on a regular contractual basis.

Here are some tips for Vlogging:

- Aim to publish regularly, once a week if you can.
- Release videos on a set day of the week and let your audience know in the video which day you broadcast.
- Plan a schedule but be flexible too so you can include content about current trends and news.
- Create enough video content that you can still deliver when you are on vacation.

- If you know what your audience like, you can also publish quality content from other channels to your subscribers.
- Create content around calendar events which are relevant to your audience.

Industry Statistics

For B2B businesses using statistics as a subject for a video can be very effective. People love statistics especially when they are dressed up to look interesting, they also love to share them too! Statistics provide knowledge and certainty about facts, they also provide a foundation for people to base their business ideas and models around. Putting a video together with interesting statistics can be as easy as putting a power point presentation together and adding narration and some royalty free music. If you don't want to stand in front of the camera then these types of video are perfect and can go viral too!

Q & A videos

Providing the answers to questions that your audience have asked can be an invaluable way of building trust and uploading this type of video on a regular basis can create quite a loyal following. Done well can this type of video can help to position you as an expert and build authority around your subject. Once you start posting your videos you may find that other questions arise from your subscribers and you can then use these as subject material for your next video.

Tutorials & how to videos

More and more people are coming to YouTube to learn how to do certain tasks and if you put a query into Google then you will find numerous YouTube videos appearing in the search results. These types of videos are incredibly useful when building your brand and very helpful in generating and capturing new leads for your business.

Product demonstration videos

Product demonstration videos are a great way to capture your product's best features while also entertaining your audience especially if your video manages to capture your enthusiasm about your products. When creating your video you need to remember you are first selling yourself so you need to be professional, clear, brief and to the point about what you want to say.

New product videos/promotional videos

Product videos definitely belong on your website however even though you do not want to keep shouting about your product, keeping your subscribers updated occasionally on your new products is a good idea especially if they are done in an entertaining way.

Entertaining/fun viral videos

Entertaining videos help to build your brand's personality and if you are lucky enough to produce a viral video you can increase your visibility massively.

Employee videos

Introducing your staff helps to give an insider view of your business and build a connection with your audience. It's a great way to create an emotional connection with your business and makes your business more transparent, approachable and friendly.

Event videos

If you are producing an event or exhibiting at a trade show or exhibition then an inspiring video about the event is a great way to show your event to those people who could not attend and is also a very effective form of promotion for your next event. Telling a story with your video is very effective way of adding interest and can help to create an emotional connection with your audience.

Customer Testimonials

What better way to promote your business than having people saying nice things about your product or service!

Explainer Videos

Explainer videos are just that and they explain what your business is about and can be either animated or live action. Explainer videos should be about 1 – 2 minutes long and belong on your website but there is no harm in adding it to your channel for your subscribers to view if they wish. You can now create inexpensive animated videos with user friendly services like www.goanimate.com which you can use to create very professional videos.

TIPS FOR CREATING EXCEPTIONAL VIDEOS

The subject and the content of your video is going to be a major contribution to making your video compelling enough for your audience to watch. However there are still certain things you can do to help create exceptional videos from pre-production stage through to uploading your video. As a general rule 80% of the work involved in creating your video needs to go into the pre-production/planning stage. Here are some of the things you need to do and think about when creating your videos:

Study other videos for inspiration and ideas

The point of this is not to copy but to inspire and get you thinking how you can use certain techniques and adapt them to your videos. Try and watch as many videos as possible which are similar to the ones you are planning and take note of the ones which have been particularly good at gaining your attention and how they have done that.

What is your goal

Your goal is the first thing you need to think about . What is the point of the video, what do you want to gain from the video and what action do you want your audience to take at the end of the video.

Figure out your story

Every video needs to tell a story so you will need to figure out what your story is going to be about, who or what will be the focus of the story and where it is going to take place. Like any story it needs to have a beginning, middle and end. The beginning is the most important and if you do not grab your audience's attention in the first couple of seconds or they will simply switch off. YouTube statistics show that the first fifteen seconds is where your viewers are most likely to drop off. So before you go any further you need to ask your yourself these questions:

- What does my audience want most?
- What do they want to know?
- What do they need?
- How can I emotionally connect with my audience?

To hook your audience you need to make your first shot intriguing, you need to address your audience and introduce them to what they are about to watch. Asking a question at the beginning of your video can be a really effective way of igniting your audience's curiosity.

Choose your location

Shooting outdoors not only adds interest to your video but also allows you to benefit from natural light. If you are shooting inside then make sure you have a clean uncluttered background, that you or the area is well lit and you have either a good source of natural light or a light source behind your camera or webcam. If you are going to be creating video content regularly then it is definitely worth investing in some proper lighting and a back drop which will really help to make your videos look professional.

Plan it out

Even if your video is just thirty seconds long it is a good idea to create a storyboard. A story board helps you to map out the order of events and who and what is going to be on camera. There are storyboard apps that you can download for android and iphone which can help you with this process. If you are employing a production team then a storyboard will help you to communicate and convey your ideas to them.

Write your script

Make a script, or at least create a list of points you need to remember and make sure you include your keywords in the script in order to optimise your video for search. Make sure you keep your script interesting throughout, your main aim is to engage, interest and entertain your audience.

Keep it short and simple

There are exceptions to this rule but for the most part it's best to keep your message short and simple and try not to cram too much information into one video by keeping to one subject, you can always make another video if you have more content. You need to get to the point quickly and deliver your message without wasting any time. Your viewers are hungry for information, so make sure you give them what they want without too much fluff. If you take too long to get to the point your viewer will simply switch off and go elsewhere. Your video length needs to be as long as it keeps your viewers interested so do not try to stretch it out just to make it longer.

Prepare and practice

Preparation and practicing in front of the camera are important. You can purchase inexpensive teleprompters which work with ipads and there are also apps available to download on iphone and android devices that let you read off a script whilst looking directly at the camera.

Use a microphone

If you are creating your own video with either your webcam or a camera it is worthwhile investing in a microphone. People are very unforgiving when it comes to bad sound.

Filming

To make your video as interesting as possible use different camera angles.

Editing

When it comes to editing it is a good idea to map it out on paper first and then pick only the most necessary and best clips. YouTube's own video editor offers you tools to combine multiple videos and images to create new videos, trim your uploads to customisable lengths, add audio and customise clips with special tools and effects. You can also add transitions and other graphics to make your video more interesting.

Add a call to action

In order to succeed on YouTube you need to get your viewers to take an action and to do this you need to prompt them by adding a strong, clear and specific call to action at the end of your video. You can ask them go to a specific landing page with your special offer to capture their email address, ask them to like, share or comment or ask them to subscribe with clear instructions on how to subscribe. In order to get your audience to take action it helps to deliver your call to action by talking directly to the camera. You can also add graphics to encourage people to subscribe and by using spotlight annotations you can make these graphics clickable. If you want to encourage your audience to comment then asking them a question and asking them to comment is a very effective way of encouraging engagement.

Add YouTube annotations to your video

Annotations are a way of adding interactive content to your videos. YouTube have made it incredibly easy to overlay text, add clickable links and they also allow you to add background information to your videos. Simply click the down arrow next to 'Upload' at the top of your account and then click on 'Video Manager,' then next to the thumbnail of your video click 'Edit' and then 'Annotations.' There are five types of annotations to choose from, speech bubble, spotlight, note, title, and label.

Use keywords in your filename

To help optimise your video for search you need to include the keywords in your filename when uploading, this tells YouTube and Google what the video is all about and will increase the chances of getting found.

Add your keywords to your title and description

Make sure the title of your video begins with your keywords and then add a secondary keyword to expand on the title. For example, Video Marketing - A guide to video marketing on YouTube. When it comes to adding your description the more text the better, between 200 – 400 words is optimal, make sure you write a useful and interesting description, while at the same time including all your possible keyword variations without obvious keyword stuffing which Google doesn't like.

Add your website link or landing page link

Make sure your website link, link to your email capture page, or a link to your special offer is on the first line of your video description. You can also add the link to your video and your channel to the bottom of the description.

Tags

Add your main keywords and your channel name too. Adding your channel name means that all of your videos will get grouped together in the related videos field. When adding tags try to be as specific as possible and don't go overboard, you want your content to be found by the right audience who are searching for your particular content.

Upload a transcript of your video

This transcript is a word for word description of what you say in your video, this is incredibly important as it communicates to Google and YouTube exactly what your video is about and will help you get your video ranked favourably. You can upload a transcript under the 'Captions' tab of your video in the 'Video Manager'. You will be offered two choices, one to transcribe and sync and one to upload a file. You can add your own transcript but it can save time if you outsource this job and then upload a .txt file. You can find people who can do this on sites like

Fiverr.com or simply type 'video transcription services' into Google search. When you have uploaded your file YouTube will sync your transcript file with your video.

Use custom thumbnails for your videos

YouTube will either choose a thumbnail, or for some users in some areas they can choose their own. YouTube are slowly rolling out this feature to everyone. One very good way of attracting viewers is to overlay title text to a desirable shot from your video. This way your potential viewers will see exactly what they are going to get and will be more likely to watch. To upload your own thumbnail simply go to the down arrow next to 'Upload' at the top of the page then click on 'Video Manager' and then click on the 'Edit' button next to your video. Under your three thumbnails images click custom thumbnail. If you do not have that option then it just means that YouTube have not introduced this is your area yet but you will have it in time.

Add a standard introduction to your videos

If you are going to be regularly uploading videos then branding every video with a standard introduction (no more than about five seconds) can be a very effective way of helping your audience identify with your brand and gives your channel a feel of professionalism and consistency. However there are two schools of thought about this and some people just see introductions as a waste of their time especially if they are regularly watching your videos. As an alternative to a standard introduction you can give a quick introduction of yourself with each video and give a brief introduction to the topic. Keeping to a fairly standard introduction script will in itself help to offer a consistent and professional experience for your viewers and will help with your branding. Another way of keeping your viewers interested with an introduction is to start with a quick introduction to your subject before your standard introduction. Starting with a question can be a great way to hook your audience. There are many ways you can get an introduction created for your video, either through a video production company or inexpensively through sites like like Fiverr.com or Splasheo.com .

CREATING HANGOUTS ON AIR

YouTube Live lets users livestream any event to their YouTube channel. This type of live streaming is for advanced creators and is ideal for large music, news and cultural events. To do this you will need to go to 'Channel Settings' and enable live events. However, there is another type of live event which is ideal for business use and this is with Google + Hangouts on Air. Google + 'Hangouts on Air' and 'YouTube Live' are two separate features.

Hangouts on Air enable you to live stream your Google + Hangout on your YouTube channel and your Google + homepage. If you have a Google + profile and a verified YouTube channel you will be able to use Hangouts on Air as long as your account is in good standing.

Google + Hangouts have made everything possible in terms of connecting and broadcasting live to both individuals and groups of people on video. Anyone with a verified Google + account who has installed the plugin and has a webcam can stream Hangouts on Air live to YouTube, their Google+ profile and their website. This amazing technology has opened up numerous of opportunities for businesses to connect with their customers and prospects.

Google + Hangouts

Hangouts are found on the top right of your Google + profile and are found in green text in quotes. Google + Hangouts can be used for private video chats or video conferencing with up to 9 other people or just text chat with another person or a group of people. Hangouts are only visible to the people who are invited and are useful for groups of friends who want to communicate or for companies who want to run private meetings. They are not recorded or streamed to YouTube or your profile.

Hangouts on Air (HOA)

HOA' s are found in the drop down menu on the left of your Google + profile and you can also create a Hangout on Air from the 'Events' tab. With HOA's you can have up to 10 people participating but the difference is they are publicly viewable to an unlimited audience and they are automatically streamed to your YouTube account and your Google + profile. Having an HOA is like having your very own TV programme with the added advantage that you can actually interact with your audience, plus it's free! HOA's automatically get ranked in Google and offer you yet another way of getting found in search.

There are great benefits to using HOA's, you can run your own Webinar without incurring the high costs which are usually involved in running one and without the restrictions on audience numbers, also there is no need for viewers to download any special software to watch and listen.

One of the best things about HOA's is that they are incredibly straightforward and you need no technical knowledge to run a very professional looking meet up or presentation. You can share your screen and upload your slides from SlideShare by simply selecting the SlideShare option and you can also install a Q & A app which allows viewers to ask questions during the HOA. When you turn the Q & A app on you will see an area to the right of the HOA where your viewers can post their questions and you can answer them.

When you start your hangout and before you start broadcasting, you can take the URL and embed it on your website, blog or Facebook for live streaming. After your HOA is over it will be visible for anyone to watch, unless you choose for it not to be.

The opportunities for marketing are limitless, you don't even have to be live on camera to do an HOA, you can do a slide presentation and then stream it to YouTube. Here are a few other ideas for using HOA's:

- Run a Webinar. A huge money saving when compared to the well known online meeting services and your audience do not have to download any software either and they can ask questions if the Q & A app is installed.
- Run a press conference.
- Customer service session.
- Customer meeting especially useful for overseas customers.
- Q & A sessions.
- Product launch.
- Product demonstrations.
- Consulting sessions.
- How to videos.
- Teaching videos/ language teaching.
- Private coaching sessions.
- Give presentations / Slide shows.

Creating Google + Hangouts on Air

To create an HOA you need to make sure your computer has the supported browser (Chrome) and the minimum processing and bandwidth requirements. Most PC's and Macs will have this but it is a good idea to check in Google + Help for more information about 'Hangout system requirements'. These are the steps involved in starting and broadcasting an HOA.

- **Install Link with YouTube and verify.** When you originally click the 'Create Hangout on Air' button you will need to install the latest version of the Google + voice and video plugin. Simply follow the simple on screen instructions. In order to stream your HOA to YouTube and so that your Hangout on Air can be recorded, you will need to link your Google + page or profile to your YouTube channel. Both your Google + and YouTube account must be linked to the same Gmail account. You will then need to verify your YouTube channel which will allow you to have unlimited length videos. If you do not verify it you are limited to fifteen minutes of video. To verify your channel go to your YouTube settings and click verify and they will send you a text message with a verification code. You can start an HOA from either your Google+ page or your profile. Also when you use your page your HOA will be connected with your own personal YouTube account unless you have linked your page to a separate YouTube account.

- **Click 'Start a Hangout on Air'**

- **Name your Hangout on Air** Try to use a name that will grab your audience's attention and inspire them.

- **Now invite people from the drop down options** These can include your Google Circles, friends and family. You can't invite public (non Google+ users) to participate but they will be able to watch the Hangout broadcasting.

- **Click 'Start the Hangout'.** Your HOA will begin but you will not be broadcasting and your HOA will not be recording. You can check to see if your camera angle and lighting is all ok before you start broadcasting. This is when you can stream your HOA live on another website by embedding your Hangout link. This is found on the bottom right of the screen along with your YouTube event page and this is where people can watch your HOA. If you want to send your participants a link so they can directly link to the hangout, then you can get this from the top of the screen and then send this out by email or text.

- **Press 'Start Broadcasting'** Your broadcast will be posted live on your Google + homepage and your HOA will also run on your YouTube channel.

- **Control your Hangout on Air** When you create a hangout then you are in control of what people hear and see. You can mute people if they are noisy or you can click on a persons video to make that person appear on the main screen.

- **Open Chat** You can open up a chat window where your participants can communicate. If you want people who are just viewing to be able to communicate or chat then you can let them do that either on YouTube, the comments on your blog, or on Google +.

- **Edit your recording** You can edit your recording on YouTube when it is finished and the post will be updated on Google+ automatically.

TIPS FOR HANGOUTS ON AIR

- **Get familiar** Watch some other HOA's to get an idea of what can be achieved and what does and doesn't work.

- **Know what you want to achieve** Be clear about your marketing goals and how your audience are going to benefit as a result of hosting your HOA .

- **PLAN PLAN PLAN** Make sure you plan and know exactly what you are going to say and how you are going to present your HOA. If you are going to use slides then practice sharing your screen and using the slides. Also plan how you are going to involve and draw your participants into the HOA.

- **TEST TEST TEST** Before you start broadcasting you will need to practice and test the various features available to make yourself familiar with audio and video settings. Make sure all the screens you want to show are open and ready to share. To practice simply choose a group with no one in it, or select yourself when you select your invites and don't press 'Start Broadcast'.

- **Get hardwired** Make sure you are hardwired with your internet connection and use an ethernet cable. Wifi is just not good enough and you may experience screen freezing or other bad quality issues.

- **Screen share** If you have interesting visuals that you think your audience will benefit from then share them. You can share your screen with your audience by clicking the screen share option on the left menu and then clicking the screen you wish to share. You can also upload slides to SlideShare and share them with your audience. When you select the SlideShare option your face will appear in a small screen at the bottom of the screen while your slides show at the top. You can also share your documents on screen with Google Drive.

- **Avoid audio feedback** To avoid audio feedback (a terrible ringing or screeching noise) use a headset microphone, this will also block out noise from the tapping of a keyboard which can be very distracting for the end user. To control audio settings click on the gear icon on the top right.

- **Make sure you light up your area** Natural light is good but if you do have a light source make sure it is behind the webcam and facing you.

- **Install Google Chrome** For optimal performance it may be a good idea to install Chrome browser since it is a Google product .

- **Brand your Hangout on Air** You can brand your Hangout on Air and add your name and business name to the lower third of your screen so it is visible to your audience. You can do this with the 'Lower third app', a third party app, which is part of the 'Hangout Toolbox' and can be found on the left toolbar. If you do not see this you just go to 'View more apps' and search for 'Hangout toolbox'. You can then add your lower third text or upload a custom branded image. You can also ask your participants to do this so your audience are clear about who everyone is.

- **Be ready** Make sure you are ready and looking professional. Remember this is a live representation of your brand, so make sure your background area is tidy and bright as possible and practice your presentation skills.

- **Check your position** Make sure you are centred on the screen and that while broadcasting you need to look at the camera above your screen so it looks like you are looking at your audience and not at your screen.

- **Use hangout chat** This is found on the left menu and is used for chat within the hangout with your participants. This is not seen by the public and is not recorded. If you would like to offer the opportunity for your audience to interact and ask questions during the Hangout on Air then simply turn on the Q&A app which is found in the left column.

- **Control who is on air** Use the cameraman app to control who is on air. This is the video icon which is found when you hover over someone's thumbnail in the film strip. Participants will see anyone who has been hidden but the public will not.

- **Manage your HOA** If someone behaves inappropriately at your hangout you can simply hover over their thumbnail and eject them.

- **Mute yourself when you are not talking** Before the HOA starts ask all participants to mute their microphones when they are not speaking. As the creator of the hangout you can mute a participant if they are being noisy.

- **Edit your HOA** You can edit your video after broadcasting with the YouTube video editor. You can combine videos, trim your videos to custom lengths, add approved music and customise with special tools and effects. http://www.youtube.com/editor

- **Connect with your participants before your HOA starts** Arrange for your participants to attend twenty minutes before broadcast so you can prepare them and answer any questions before hand.

- **Leave time for Q&A's** Make sure you leave enough time at the end of the event for Q&A's.

- If you do not want your HOA to be watched you can simply delete it from your Google + profile and then make it private on your YouTube account.

PROMOTING YOUR HANGOUT ON AIR

Build your audience

Before you start creating events make sure you have built up your subscribers on YouTube. If you have a good following on Google + this is a great way to promote your HOA as well.

Promote with your embed Code

When you start your HOA you will find an embed code at the top of the hangout which you can shorten. You can embed this link into your website or blog and Facebook make sure you embed it before you hit the broadcast button!

Promote on all your social networks

Promote your HOA on your other social media networks by creating and posting a compelling image. You could use a promoted post on Facebook to make sure as many people hear about you HOA on Facebook.

Create a publicity video on YouTube

Create a sort teaser video about what the Hangout on Air is going to be about to create some buzz about the event. You can create a short 'Hype' Video at http://www.hypemyhangout.com/

Optimise on YouTube for after event views

Make sure you optimise your video on YouTube. Simply visit your video manager and make sure you fill in your description and use all your keywords so this broadcast keeps getting found long after it has been broadcasted.

Send out emails

Send out invitations to your email contacts and you opt-in list and your LinkedIn connections if you are on LinkedIn.

Advertise it on your website or blog

Add an image or text to your blog advertising your online event .

Advertise on Google Adwords

By advertising your event with Google Adwords and using keywords that will catch your target audience you can grow following on Google +.

Ask your participants to promote it

Ask your participants to invite their Circles and share your promotional images. You could also ask them to add any promotional images to their website or Blog and encourage them to write a blog post about the subject and HOA.

Schedule and publicise your Hangout on Air with an event on Google + .

If you have already got an audience on Google + then you can schedule your HOA and let your audience know about it well in advance, simply click on the 'Events' tab, then 'Event Options' and then 'Advanced' and then click on 'Make this an Event on Air' (this is usually used for offline public events) then click on 'Show more options' where you will be able to add more detailed information. Make sure you make it clear that the event is an online event. Google + does not give you the URL of your HOA until you have started it. However, there is a simple way around this, you can either add the URL for your Google + homepage or add your YouTube UR for the Hangout on Air, http://www.youtube.com/user/*username*/live (Replace username with the name of your youtube account.) This way people will be directed to your YouTube account where the hangout on air will be streaming. Make sure you are specific about the time of your 'Hangout on Air' so that when your attendees arrive at the address, the 'Hangout on Air' is taking place, otherwise they will be directed to the homepage.

Add a good image promoting the Hangout on Air and complete the event form with all the information. You can then select who you want to invite and the Hangout will appear on Google Calendar for anyone who uses it.

Create some buzz
Start talking about your event or Hangout 4 −5 Days before the date and post an image.

Google + Communities
Sharing information about your HOA on any relevant Google + Communities that you are a member of will be a good way of getting people to watch your HOA.

Share on SlideShare

After your event has taken place you can upload it to SlideShare which will help to drive additional traffic.

Chapter Five

Building your Audience on YouTube

IN ORDER TO leverage the power of YouTube you will need subscribers. You will need to build an audience of loyal viewers who want to keep coming back for your compelling content. In addition to optimising your videos for search, having subscribers who regularly watch your videos is going to be a major contribution to getting your videos ranked highly in both Google and YouTube search. Having people viewing, favoriting, commenting and liking your videos is all going to help with your YouTube ranking. Here are some essential strategies for getting you more subscribers on YouTube:

Post content regularly

In order to create a successful channel and attract regular subscribers your will need to post video content regularly and keep to a regular schedule. Many businesses get discouraged when they don't immediately get hundreds of views on their channel but this is normal and it will take time to build your views unless of course, you have instantly managed to create viral content.

Ask for subscribers

At the end of each video you need to ask your viewers to subscribe, give them a reason why they should subscribe and let them know how to do it. You can also ask them to add a comment, or like your video. If you ask you usually get ! Don't forget you can use annotations and include a clickable subscribe link in your video itself but make sure you give your viewers enough time to complete the action before the video finishes.

Subscribe & interact with other channels

If you subscribe to other similar channels and interact with those channels you are likely to get reciprocal subscriptions and other subscribers are more likely to like, comment or share your content. Responding to comments and questions will help to build relationships and will show that you value your subscribers.

Cross promotion & collaboration

By working with other creators you can cross promote your content with other channels who have similar audiences, this is a great way to widen your reach and attract new audiences. Creating Hangouts on Air with other channel owners and recording video chats with other channels can also really help to increase your exposure to new audiences.

Add featured channels

Featured channels show on the right hand side of your channel. This is where you can add a link to other channels you like. This is a great way to build relationships with people who have similar audiences and hopefully they will reciprocate by adding your channel to their featured channels.

Optimise your videos

Make sure your title, descriptions and tags are completed and optimised properly, that you add a transcript and choose the best thumbnail image for your video.

Link your channel with Google+

Google + creates another place for your videos to be discovered. If you already have a YouTube channel then it is a very good idea to link it with Google +. You can engage your subscribers with Google Hangouts and broadcast them live on your YouTube channel with Hangouts on Air. When anyone comments on any of video of yours, it will appear in their feed in Google+ which will help to widen your reach on Google +

Please note if you already have a Google + account and a YouTube channel and you disconnect these, you will not be able to leave comments on other peoples videos.

Add YouTube subscribe button

You can choose which subscribe button you want to add to your website. The instructions how to do this are at this page https:// developers.google.com/youtube/youtube_subscribe_button.

Promote your channel

Promote your channel at every opportunity, on your blog, website and other social media platforms, use Facebook promoted posts, and add your videos to your blog posts and articles. Submitting your video to Stumbleupon has proved a powerful means of getting your site found.

Advertise on YouTube

With Adwords for video you only pay to have your video viewed and it's a great way to get the ball rolling and build a following. You can reach your targeted audience based on where they live, what they are interested in and their gender. Your ads can drive comments, likes, subscriptions and comments.

Send to your email list

Inviting your current opt-in subscribers to subscribe to your YouTube channel is another way to grow your reach and continue to build trust and rapport.

Promote your video on SlideShare

The ability to upload videos on SlideShare as well as presentations is still under utilised by its users. Getting views and exposure on SlideShare for any business related video is quite likely to be viewed by more people on SlideShare than on YouTube. If you are uploading to YouTube then make sure you upload to SlideShare as well.

CHAPTER SIX

DAY TO DAY ACTIVITY

THERE ARE CERTAIN things that you will need to do on a day to day basis to successfully run your campaign on YouTube. It is a good idea to allot a specific amount of time and a particular time of the day to do this. Here are some of the things you will need to do:

Subscribing to your customer channels

This is important if your customers are business owners themselves. Subscribing to their channels will go a long way in building relationships. By subscribing you are showing them that you are interested in what they have to say and also helping them to achieve their goals by helping them to build their audience.

Respond to comments

When your subscribers start to engage with your content, make sure you are listening and responding to them. There is nothing worse than going to a YouTube channel where subscribers have taken the time to ask questions and then have not been responded to by the channel owner. Answering and responding to comments not only helps to build relationships but also helps to build trust and authenticity for your business.

Showing your audience you value and respect them

If you value and respect your audience they will most probably love, respect and value your business. Be kind, generous, offer as much help and value as possible, reply to their comments and make it obvious that you value them and are listening to them. Don't be afraid to be yourself rather than a stiff brand with no personality. Be friendly to your audience, be chatty, authentic, genuine and embrace the conversation. All this will all go a long well in building a positive image for your brand and will set you apart from your others who are continually ambushing their audience with self promotion.

Everyone is aiming for shares, likes and comments so if you are helping others out by commenting and liking their content it is going to draw attention to your brand and they are more likely to take an interest in your content. This is one area where the reciprocation rule works very well on YouTube. Engaging with content will also draw attention to you and your brand and you will find that people will click on your name to find out who you are and they may very well subscribe to your channel.

Following influencers in your niche
Building relationships with key influencers in your niche is invaluable. Not only can you learn from their content but also these people can have literally thousands of subscribers, imagine if they subscribe to your channel and then share your content!

Dealing with negative comments
Every business at some time will have to deal with negativity from followers. Hopefully if you have a good product then this is not going to happen too often. There are the 'trolls' out there who have nothing better to do than post negative comments, the best thing to do with them is just ignore them, delete their comments and block them if they really become a problem. However there will be real customers who have real concerns and complaints and may post negative comments publicly, there may also be people who really want to lash out to gain your attention as quickly as possible and spread the news to their friends too! You need to deal with these complaints as quickly as possible and be as transparent and authentic as possible. The best thing to do is to apologise and say how sorry you are to hear of the inconvenience they have been caused and offer to continue the conversation and deal with their concern by

either private message or telephone. You can then deal with this privately, give your customer the full attention they deserve and decide on your next course of action or compensation.

CHAPTER SEVEN

MEASURING AND MONITORING YOUR RESULTS

MEASURING AND MONITORING your results and performance against your original goals and objectives on a continual basis is essential. This is where many businesses go wrong, they carry on aimlessly posting content without checking to see what is working and what is not. Then after 6 months or a year they wonder why their campaign is making no positive difference at all.

When you measure your results you will discover so much information about your campaign which will allow you to steer your campaign in the right direction to achieve those SMART goals and objectives and stop anything that is not working.

When you originally plan your content and work out your strategies and tactics for your campaign you will be estimating what you need to do to achieve your goals and objectives. However, as you campaign develops will have a better idea of what you need to do to achieve your goals and objectives. For example, you may need to increase the amount you spend on advertising to attract new subscribers, or you may need to create more content around a certain subject that you have found to be very popular. This is what it is all about, making your campaign work for you by constantly measuring your success against the goals set and then adjusting your strategies accordingly in order to achieve the results.

YOUTUBE ANALYTICS

YouTube Analytics provides you with a wealth of information to measure your campaign and your performance and shows you data about your earning, engagement, traffic sources and more. Analytics provides filters which help you sort by content, geography and date. You can find out whether a video is popular in a certain region or look at its performance over a specific period of time. Analytics are found under the gear icon on the top right and you can view and download the following reports:

The Overview Report

The overview report shows you how your content is performing on YouTube and shows you the number of views and the estimated minutes watched for the channel and for individual videos. It shows engagement metrics including likes, comments and shares and your top ten most viewed videos. It shows demographic information about the gender and location of your viewers and also the top traffic sources for your videos.

The Views Report

The views report displays data about the views and estimated minutes watched.

The Devices Report

The devices report shows information about the different devices and operating systems that viewers use to watch your videos.

The demographics Report

Displays information about the gender and age of your audience. You can alter the date range and geographic location to see how the audience varies.

Audience Retention Reports

The Audience Retention report is a measure of your videos ability to keep its audience. It is a graph which displays data for both organic traffic and paid traffic and shows the following:

- **Absolute Audience Retention:** The views of every moment of your video as a percentage of views. You can see for instance on the graph if viewers have rewatched a video, if they have started watching midway through the video or if the video has been abandoned or fast forwarded. If you discover that people have stopped watching at a particular point then you can make a change for the better. The first fifteen seconds is probably the most important part to keep an eye on for drop off.

- **Relative Audience Retention:** This shows your video's capacity to retain viewers during playback in comparison to all YouTube videos of similar length. The higher the graph at a given moment the more viewers kept watching your video over the previous seconds of playback compared against other videos at the same moment in their playbacks.

The Engagement Report

Engagement reports are a great way to understand your audience's interest and show you how users are integrating with your channel by displaying the number of likes, dislikes, favourites, comments and shares.

Traffic Sources Reports

The traffic resources report shows you the various sources through which your content was found. There are numerous ways your videos could be found, through YouTube or Google search, through other social networking websites like Google +,Twitter, LinkedIn and Facebook.

The Earnings Report

This is for partners who are using YouTube to earn money through Adsense and show your total number of views and estimated earnings.

GOOGLE ANALYTICS

Google Analytics will be able to give you detailed information about the impact YouTube is having on your business and provides advanced reports that will let you track the effectiveness of your campaign with the following social reports:

The Overview Report This report lets you see at a glance how much conversion value is generated from social channels. It compares all conversions with those conversions resulting from social.

The Conversions Report The conversions report helps you to quantify the value of social and shows conversion rates and the monetary value of conversions that occurred due to referrals from YouTube and any of the other social networks. Google Analytics can link visits from YouTube with the goals you have chosen and your E - commerce transactions. To do this you will need to configure your goals in Google Analytics which is found under 'Admin' and then 'Goals'. Goals in Google Analytics let you measure how often visitors take or complete a specific action and you can either create goals from the templates offered or create your own custom goals.

The Conversions report can be found in the Standard Reporting tab under Traffic Sources > Social > Conversions.

The Networks Referral Report The Networks Referral report tells you how many visitors the social networks have referred to your website and shows you how many page views, visits, the duration of the visits and the average number of pages viewed per visit. From this information you can determine which network referred the highest quality of traffic.

Data Hub Activity Report The Data Hub activity report shows how people are engaging with your site on the social networks . You can see the most recent URL's that were shared, how they were shared and what was said.

The Social Visitors Flow Report This report displays the initial paths that your visitors took from social sites through to your site and where they exited.

The Landing Pages Report This report displays engagement metrics for each URL. These include page views, average visit duration and pages viewed per visit.

The Trackbacks Report The Trackback report shows you which sites are linking to your content and how many visits those sites are sending to you. This can help you to work out which sort of content is the most successful so you can create similar and it also helps you to build relationships with those who are constantly linking to your content.

CHAPTER EIGHT

BUILDING YOUR BRAND ON YOUTUBE

YOUR MAIN AIM through this whole process is going to be to connect, capture and convert your prospects through your website or blog, through YouTube and through other social networks and this involves the following:

- **Connect** Your product needs to be the connection between your prospect and what they need so the first thing you need to do is connect those two things. In order to do this you need to identify who they are, find them out of all the millions of people on the internet and then connect with them by offering them something they want or need.

- **Capture** Once you have found them you need to capture them on your website, blog, YouTube or any other social media platforms. This is so you can continue your relationship with them either by email or through YouTube and continue to communicate your brand message. To do this you need to offer them some sort of incentive so you can capture their name and email address.

- **Convert** When you have captured your prospect you need to convert them into a paying customer by nurturing them and continuing to build a relationship by offering them the content they want through email and YouTube and then moving them toward signing up for a special or exclusive offer.

To achieve this successfully you are going to need to have a well defined brand and that brand needs to be communicated through everything you do or say through YouTube, through your website, blog and your email campaign.

Whether you are a one person small business, large corporation or an organisation, your brand is one of the most important attributes of your business. Your brand is what you want your prospects and customers to respect, trust and fall in love with so they will buy and continue to buy your products and services. Your brand is what is going to set you apart from any other business and what will give your business the competitive edge.

Never has there been a better time for your business to build your brand and communicate your brand message to your target audience than through YouTube. Your brand is the main ingredient for success and YouTube is giving you the channel to communicate it. You can literally communicate with your audience everyday and if you get it right and connect the right brand experience with the right target audience you are onto an all round winner.

It may be that you have a well established brand already, maybe you have not created your brand yet or it just needs some tweaking or fine tuning. Maybe you are not exactly sure what your brand is, or maybe you feel it needs a complete overhaul. Whatever your situation is, you need to know that your brand is going to underpin your whole YouTube campaign and it needs to be strong, clear, well defined and consistent. Once defined your business is going to create it, be it, communicate it, display it, picture it, speak it, promote it and most of all be true to it. This chapter is going to take you through everything you need know and do to define and create your brand so you can get into the hearts and minds of your target audience by communicating the right message and brand experience.

There are many definitions of the word brand but this is the one I like best because it incorporates pretty much all the necessary information you will need to help you to define your own brand.

Brand, the definition

Your brand is more than a name, symbol or logo, it is your commitment and your promise to your customer. Your brand is the defined personality of either yourself as an individual brand or your product, service, company or organisation, it's what sets you apart and differentiates your business from your competition and any other business. Your brand is created and influenced by your vision and everything you stand for including; people, visuals, culture, style, perception, words, messages, PR, opinions, news media, and especially, social media.

Why is your brand so important to your business?

Branding is important because it helps you and your business build and create powerful and lasting relationships by communicating everything you want to say about your product or service to your prospects and customers. A strong brand encourages loyalty and will ultimately create a strong customer base and increase your sales by doing the following:

- Demonstrating to your prospects and customers that you are professional and committed to offering them what you promise.
- Making your business easily recognisable.
- Creating a clear distinction from your competition.
- Making your business memorable.
- Creating an emotional attachment with your audience.
- Helping to create trust.
- Helping to build customer loyalty and repeat custom.
- Creating a valuable asset which will be financially beneficial if you sell your business.
- Creating a competitive advantage.

To do all the above you are going to have to find a way to get into the hearts and minds of your customers so they will ultimately buy and continue to buy your products or services. Before launching your campaign and setting up profiles, posting content and engaging, you will need to have a clear picture of exactly what your brand is, or what you want your brand to be. You will need to define exactly how your brand is perceived now, how you want your brand to be perceived, where your business fits into the market, who your target audience is and how you want your business to develop in the future.

To do this you need a deep understanding of your business and the people who are going to be most interested in your products and how you are going to serve them. When it comes to defining your ideal target audience you need to work out which of your products are the most popular and which are the most profitable so you can focus your efforts in finding and connecting with the right audience and then creating the right brand experience for them.

YOUR VISION/YOUR STORY

If you want to create a strong brand then when of the first things you need to do is create a clear visual picture of how you see your business now and in the future. This is about daring to see what your business could be without constraints or limitations.

This exercise will not only help you to work out what you want to achieve financially and creatively but also makes you focus on what really matters and will help you to create your own unique voice and story. This is incredibly important when it comes to your branding as this is what is going to make your business stand out from others and give you that edge.

To do this you need to get away from all distractions and think about how you would like to see your business grow and develop in the next three years. This is more than just putting a mission statement together, this is about your core business beliefs, why you are doing it, what you want your business to be and how you want to be perceived in your market. To help you do this you will need to ask yourself the following questions and record your answers:

- Why did you originally start your business or why are you starting a business?
- How did your original business idea come about?
- What changes are you looking to make in peoples lives?
- What are you hoping to achieve?
- What aspects of your business are really important to you?
- What are your hopes and dreams?
- What is your definition of success?
- What sort of turnover and income defines that success?
- How many employees does your business have?
- Why are you in business?
- What are your core values in your business?
- What impact do you want to have?
- What influence do you want to have?
- What sort of things do you want the media saying about you?
- What do you want your customers to be saying about you ?
- How you want to be portrayed on social media?
- How many YouTube subscribers do you want ?
- What markets are you in? Are you local, national or international?

Once you have completed this exercise you will have all the material you need so that you can create the unique experience required to make your business stand out from all the others in your niche. This is the first step towards creating a brand for your business, this is the beginning of your story.

DEFINING YOUR BRAND

Whether you are responsible for defining, creating and developing your brand in-house, or you are employing a local branding and marketing agency, you will need to carry out an analysis of your business to define your brand. Completing the following exercise will help you to define and find clarity about your brand:

- A factual description of what your business is and the purpose of your business.

- Describe your product or service in one sentence ?

- List all your products and/or services.

- What are the benefits and features of all of your products?

- Which are your most profitable products/services?

- Which are your most popular products/services?

- Who are your ideal customers for each of your products or services? (Consumer or business, age, gender, income, occupation, education, stage in family life cycle.)

- Out of these customers who are the ones who are most likely to buy your most profitable products?

- Is the market and demand large enough to provide you with the number of customers you need to buy your most profitable products and achieve your financial goals?

- If your answer to the previous question is no then ask yourself the same question for each of your other products.

- Who are your three main competitors? (Have a look at their YouTube account.)

- What distinguishes your business from your competition? What special thing are you bringing to the market that is of real value? What is your unique selling point? What solutions are your products offering your customers that will meet their needs or solve their problems?

- If you are already in business then write down what your customers are already saying about your business. What do think they would say about how your product or service makes them feel emotionally (you may need to ask your customers if you do not already know). What qualities and words would you use to describe the personality of your business as it is now. Here are some examples of words you may wish to use: high cost, low cost, high quality, value for money, expensive, cheap, excellent customer service, friendly, professional, happy, serious, innovative, eccentric, quiet, loud, beautiful, relaxing, motivating, sincere, adventurous, amusing, charming, decisive, kind, imaginative, proactive, intuitive, loving, trustworthy, extrovert, vibrant, transparent, intelligent, creative, dynamic, resourceful.

- Now whether you are already in business or starting out write down all the words to describe how you want and need your brand to be perceived and what qualities you want to be associated with your brand in order to match the needs and expectations of your ideal customers. If you are already in business hopefully this will be exactly the same from how you perceive you are at the current time.

- What is the evidence that backs up what you have said about your brand, this could be customer testimonials or any evidence about product or service quality.

- What is the biggest opportunity for your business right now?

- What products are you thinking of introducing in the near

future?

HOW TO GET INTO THE MINDS AND HEARTS OF YOUR TARGET AUDIENCE

Your target audience is your most important commodity as they are your future customers and ambassadors of your business. Every single one of them is valuable and every single one of them can make a difference to your business. This can be because they are actually going to buy your products or simply spread the word by interacting with you on YouTube.

However it's a big social world out there, the possibilities of finding new people are limitless but targeting everyone is not the solution. The biggest mistake you can make is trying to reach everyone and then not appealing to anyone. Your first step is to identify exactly who the people are who are going to be interested in your products or services and then you need to find out everything about them. You need to get inside their heads and work out what motivates these people, what they are interested in, what their needs, hopes, aspirations and fears are and what are their dreams. Your product or service is the link between them and what they want. When you know this you can tailor every single message or piece of content towards them.

When you know exactly who your ideal customers are, YouTube offers you the opportunity to go and find and reach them. It's then up to you to capture them so you can continue to communicate with them. When you know everything about your customers you are more likely to speak the right language to be able to communicate with them and build trust to the point where the next natural progression is for them to buy your product.

It's only when you truly understand your audience you can start converting them into customers. Once you know you are targeting the right audience, you can confidently focus every ounce of your effort creating exactly the right content, nurturing them, engaging with them and looking after them. It's only a matter of time before they will buy your product.

Creating your ideal customer persona or avatar

The following exercise is absolutely essential and your answers to the questions will be the very information that is going to help you communicate with your customer in the right way, by providing them with the right content and the correct brand experience. Once you have done this exercise you are going to own some very powerful information. If you do not do this exercise it is very unlikely that you are going to be able to truly connect with your target audience in the way that is necessary to build trust so that you can ultimately convert them into your customers.

Your answers to the questions in the previous section will have given you a clear idea of which types of customers you need to target to give you the best chance of achieving your financial goals. You now need to find out everything about them so you can get your brand into their hearts and minds. The best way to do this is to create an imaginary persona or avatar of your ideal customer and you can build this picture by finding out the following:

- Describe your ideal customer and include the following details, are they a consumer or in business, their age, gender, income, occupation, education, stage in family life cycle.
- Where do they live?
- What do they want most of all?
- What are their core values ?
- What is their preferred lifestyle?
- What do they do on a day to day basis?
- What are their hopes and aspirations?
- What important truth matters to them ?
- What motivates and inspires them?

- What sort of routines do they have?
- What are their day to day priorities?
- How do they have fun?
- What do they do in their spare time?
- What subjects are they interested in?
- Which books do they read?
- Which TV programmes do they watch?
- What magazines do they read?
- Who do they follow on social media?
- Who are their role models?
- What really makes them tick?
- What are their fears and frustrations?
- What are their suspicions?
- What are their insecurities?
- What are their typical worries?
- What is the perfect solution to their worries?
- What are their dreams?
- What do they need to make them feel happy and fulfilled?

Big Questions

To answer the following questions you will need to step inside your ideal customers mind and imagine you are them.

- How do you feel when you find your product or service? What is your initial emotional reaction ?
- What are the words that go through your head?
- How can I justify buying this product for myself?
- Are you ready to buy immediately?
- Do you have any suspicions that the product may not be what it says?
- What are those suspicions? And why do you have them?
- Do you need more convincing?
- What do you need to convince you that the product is right for you?

- What do you feel when you have the product in your hand?

The reason why these are such big questions is because your answers to them will establish whether or not you have correctly defined your ideal customer and whether you have really understood their needs, desires and fears. If you are imagining yourself as your ideal customer and you are saying woohoo, ecstatically jumping up and down with glee, immediately buying the product or relieved that you have at long last found the solution to your problem, then you have created the right avatar. If not then you need to think again.

It's only when you have imagined yourself in the hearts and minds of your target audience that you are going to be able to connect with them on any emotional level. With the information from the above exercise you will have everything you need to produce exactly the right content to match the needs, desires and expectations of your ideal customer so that you can create the right brand experience and sell your products. This information is like gold.

COMMUNICATING YOUR BRAND

Once you are clear about what your brand is, who your target audience is and where you want your business to go, you will be ready to translate all this into your brand. Your brand needs to be consistent and extend to every aspect of your business, everything you do, everything you produce to promote your business and everything you say. It will also need to be evident throughout your social media campaign.

When you are clear about what your brand is, what it stands for and how you are going to stand out from other similar businesses you then need to work out how you can communicate this message in the best possible way. Your main aim here is to create an emotional connection with your target audience that is going to help them grow to love your brand, remember your brand and remain loyal to it. To do this you need to communicate your brand story through every aspect of your business including your social media campaign.

With the information you now have you are armed with everything you need to create a consistent brand and if you have not already done so you can either hand all this information over to a marketing agency or use it yourself to create all the following:

- **Your Logo** Your logo will give a clear guideline for all your promotional material including your website or blog, stationery, templates or any marketing material that needs to be created for online or offline promotion.

- **Your brand message** The main message you want to communicate about your brand.

- **Your tagline** A short, memorable statement about your brand that captures the personality of your brand and communicates how you or your product will benefit your customer.

- **All your 'about' descriptions** You can communicate your brand story through all your 'about' sections on all your social media platforms you are using.

- **The content you create for your business** Every piece of content you create for your business needs to be tailor-made for your target audience. You will need to pick who and what subjects or topics you want to be associated with your brand, as anything you pick to write about will be a representation of your brand.

- **Your website and/or blog** The about page of your website is probably the most visited page of any website and there is a reason for this, people want to find out about your business and they want to find out what is different or special about it. This is a great place to introduce and expand on the story of your brand, this is where you can really go to town and communicate your beliefs and how you are unique. Also the visual style of your website or blog and your unique voice should be evident throughout your site and be consistent with your brand.

- **Video content** Videos are an incredibly powerful way of creating a personal connection with your audience. Make sure you that whatever video content you produce and whatever you say is always consistent with your brand.

CHAPTER NINE

THE ESSENTIAL YOUTUBE MARKETING PLAN

BEFORE LAUNCHING INTO your campaign you will need to know exactly what you want your business to achieve and what you want to achieve through marketing your business on YouTube. Without the necessary planning and preparation your campaign is very unlikely to succeed.

This next few chapters take you thorough everything you need to do plan your campaign before actually posting content. In this chapter you will learn how to create your mission statement, set goals and objectives and plan the strategies and tactics you need to implement, to achieve those goals. In the following chapter you will learn exactly how to prepare your business, your website and blog and your email campaign so you can capture and convert.

CREATING YOUR MISSION STATEMENT

Many campaigns fail at the first hurdle simply because they do not have a clear idea about why they are undertaking a campaign or what they want to achieve. They set up a YouTube Account and have little or no idea why exactly they are doing it, "Everyone else is doing it... we probably should too" Then they launch in without first articulating the purpose of their YouTube campaign and aimlessly start posting content. Before long they realise that this is having no positive effect on their business and either give up or continue half heartedly.

Once you have defined your brand and your target audience you will need to produce your mission statement for your YouTube campaign. Your mission statement is vital for your business as a whole and for your prospects and customers and should clearly state your commitment and promise to them as well as communicating your brand message. You will be able to include this in your YouTube channel description. To create your mission statement simply follow these for four easy steps:

- **Describe what your business does** Describe exactly what you do and what you offer and the purpose of your business.

- **Describe the way you operate** Include your core values, your level of customer service, your commitment to your customers. You can include how your core values contribute to the quality of your product or service

- **Who are you doing it for?** Who are your customers? Business owners, entrepreneurs, working women, gardeners, shop owners, etc.

- **The value you are bringing** What benefit are you offering your customers? What value are you bringing them?

Once you have created your statement everyone will know exactly what you are about. You will know exactly what you need to deliver to your customers. Your employees will know what is expected of them. Your customers and prospects will know exactly what your promise is, and what they can expect when buying your products and services.

SETTING YOUR GOALS AND OBJECTIVES

Setting goals and objectives is the key to your success on YouTube. Once they are set you will be ready to plan and create the strategies and tactics to achieve those goals and objectives and you will be able to review and measure the success of your campaign.

Definition of a goal

A goal is a statement rooted in your business's mission and it will define what you want to accomplish and offer a broad direction for your business to follow. The three main goals of any business will ultimately be to increase sales, to reduce costs and to improve customer service and each goal will have a direct effect on the others. Here are some examples of goals and objectives within those three main goals:

1. To increase revenue and generate sales

- To increase website traffic.
- To increase brand awareness through YouTube.
- To build a reputation as an expert within the industry.
- To build a loyal and engaged community on YouTube.
- To increase the number of customers from word of mouth and referrals.
- To increase the number of sales.
- To increase average spend per customer.
- To increase the number of leads generated.
- To introduce new products.
- To increase online visibility.
- To promote an event.
- To build a highly targeted list of email subscribers.
- To connect with new customers.
- To build trust and build relationships with prospects and customers.
- To put a content marketing strategy in place.
- To increase business in 'X' country/state.
- To become a thought leader in your industry.
- To develop new markets by introducing your products into 'X' country/state.
- To decrease spend on traditional forms of advertising and invest 'X' amount in YouTube marketing.
- To build relationships with key influencers on YouTube.

2. To reduce Costs

- To decrease spend on traditional forms of advertising and invest in YouTube marketing.

3. To deliver customer satisfaction and retain customers

- To answer customer questions promptly.
- To respond to customer complaints promptly, politely and helpfully.
- To provide online help/technical support.
- To respond to customer feedback.
- To listen to your customers.

Setting measurable objectives

Once you set your broader goals then you need to get more specific and create SMART objectives (specific, measurable, attainable, relevant and time bound). Here is an explanation of exactly what each of those terms means:

- **Specific** You need to target particular areas for improvement.
- **Measurable** Your progress needs to be quantifiable and putting concrete figures on your goals is essential for success and is the only way to measure the effectiveness of your campaign.
- **Attainable / Realistic** You need to be realistic with the resources you have available and the results you are expecting need to be realistic.
- **Relevant** Your goals need to be relevant to the business climate you are in.
- **Time Bound** Make sure you set a realistic time period to achieve your goals. If a time is not set then things don't tend to get done.

Here are some examples of the sort of SMART objectives you should be setting:

- To find new customers on YouTube by creating compelling

content.

- To build an audience of X number subscribers on YouTube within one year.
- To increase number of Subscribers by X per week.
- To increase website traffic from YouTube by X times.
- To increase opt-in list subscribers by X per week
- Increase conversions from YouTube by X per week.
- To increase the number of leads generated from YouTube by X per week.
- To increase the number of new customers by X per month.
- To increase the average spend per customer by X.
- Introduce X number of new products every 6 months.
- To decrease spend on traditional forms of advertising by X and invest X amount in YouTube marketing.
- Utilise YouTube to increase attendants at X event by X people.
- To become a thought leader.
- To support PR by adding a video with your PR releases.
- To enhance blog posts with video.
- To support your social media goals by providing rich content for your other platforms. To capture leads from other channels to convert to sales.

CHOOSING YOUR STRATEGIES AND TACTICS

Once you have set your quantifiable goals and objectives you are going to have to work out how you are going to accomplish them using YouTube. You will need to think about the strategies and tactics you are going to use and they need to be quantifiable as well. Here are some examples of the strategies you may want to implement:

- To create compelling content, capture leads and convert with the use of and incentive, email opt-in.
- To post a video on YouTube every week on YouTube.
- To spend 'X' minutes per day liking, commenting and sharing videos on other channels.

- To follow 'X' number of influencers on YouTube per week.
- To create 'X' number of online events per year.
- To add a video to every press release that is sent out.
- To create at least one article per week on business blog and post video.
- To produce a video for every blog post to encourage more traffic from YouTube and to support the blog with video as well.
- To remarket and advertise to people who have already watched your YouTube videos, subscribed or unsubscribed to your channel with adverts on YouTube and across the Google display network.
- To spend 'X' amount on YouTube advertising.
- To upload every video to SlideShare.
- To share every video on other social platforms.
- To announce your channel on all other social platforms.

Of course at the beginning you are going to need to make an educated guess at the number of times you are going to need to do one thing to achieve another. As your campaign runs you will need to adjust certain aspects to achieve what you set out to achieve. For example, you may need to create more videos or you may need to change the type of content you are creating to increase the amount of engagement.

The only way you can do this is by constantly monitoring and measuring your results against the original goals and objectives you set and adjusting your campaign accordingly.

CREATING YOUR YOUTUBE POSTING CALENDAR

Now you have your strategies in place you will have a good idea of the amount and type of content you need to post to achieve those objectives. One of the most challenging tasks of your YouTube campaign is going to be to consistently deliver a high standard of content to your subscribers on a regular basis. This may seem daunting to begin with but you will be surprised just how one idea leads to another.

To help you map out your content for the next six months or the year ahead you need to create a YouTube posting calendar which is going to be your key to consistent posting. There are many online tools and apps that can help you with this. Google Calendar is a very good calendar to use and lets you colour code the different types of post. You can also use Hootsuite, the social media dashboard to plot out your calendar or use a spreadsheet in Excel. There are also other online applications like www.trello.com which has easy to use drag and drop features and using mind mapping applications like 'Simplemind' can really help when brainstorming for content ideas.

To get started you will simply need to map out and schedule the days of the week for each week of the year and decide what types of post you are going to create for certain days. You will need to balance the type of content in order to create variety and interest for your audience. You then need to create topics or themes and then break the year down into weeks/months and make a schedule. You can then add all the things that you are planning within your business, like offers, contests, product launches, Webinars and then add all the things going on outside your business like public holidays and special events. You then need to incorporate all that information into your daily action plan.

It may seem daunting to look at a blank calendar but you will be surprised how it comes together when you start breaking it down into months, weeks and days. A posting calendar will help you keep your campaign focused and on track and in line with your brand and your marketing goals and also keep it balanced in terms of the subject and type of media you use. A calendar will help you look ahead and help you to incorporate your marketing plan into your YouTube campaign. It may be that you are launching a new product, or maybe certain products tie in with specific holidays, you may have certain industry events you need to attend or are perhaps creating your own.

CHAPTER TEN

PREPARING YOUR BUSINESS FOR SUCCESS

WHETHER YOUR SITE is being found through organic search, an advertising campaign, YouTube or any other social media platform all your hard work is going to be wasted unless you have put a system in place to capture leads and convert them into customers. This system has to start from the moment your prospect either hits your website, your blog or your YouTube Channel and your ultimate goal is to convert your browsers into buyers.

Firstly the unfortunate fact is that the majority of your website visitors are unlikely to buy from you on their first visit and if you do not have a website that grabs their attention within the first couple of seconds then they will move very quickly onto another site. Secondly even if your site does catch their eye they are still likely to check out other sites and still may not return. To make any kind of impact at all your site needs to grab their attention and then capture their email address so you can continue your relationship with them through email. This chapter is going to take you through steps you will need to take, from getting your website or blog ready, to setting up and creating your email campaign.

Email is still one of the most powerful ways to convert prospects into customers and has a conversion rate three times higher than social media conversion rates. That is not to say that your YouTube campaign is any less important, as this is where you are going to find and nurture your leads and transfer them to your opt-in by either capturing them on YouTube or on your website or blog. This chapter is going to take you through steps you will need to take from getting your website or blog ready, to setting up and creating your email campaign.

PREPARING YOUR WEBSITE FOR SUCCESS

Whether you already have a website or blog or you are creating a new site from scratch you need to make sure it has the necessary features to grab the attention of your target audience and capture their email addresses. Capturing the email addresses of your target audience has to be one of your most important goals when creating your website. Once your prospects have voluntarily submitted their email address you have the opportunity to build a relationship, communicate your message and promote your products and services on an ongoing and regular basis. A well thought out and crafted email campaign can immediately establish trust and favour with your subscribers. Don't forget that it is you who owns your opt-in list and nobody can take it away from you and as long as you are providing your subscribers value with great content they are likely to want to keep hearing from you. Remember you cannot rely on social media to continue your relationship as these platforms are changing all the time, you need to build your email list.

Once you have completed the exercise in the branding section and have your ideal customer persona or avatar you will have a clear picture of what your target audience's pain point or problem is and how your product can help solve their problem or make their life better in some way. If you have a blog, and most businesses today need a blog, you will also have all the tools you need to create the right content to attract your target audience. Armed with this information you are half way ready to putting a system in place to sell, so your products sell themselves and your website is working like an extra sales person selling your products 24/7.

When your visitor arrives at your site you have only three seconds to grab their attention. You need to connect emotionally with them and let them know immediately that they have arrived at the right place by communicating exactly how you are going to help them and what it is you are offering them.

Once they are on your site you then need to win their interest and confidence so that they will voluntarily submit their email address. To do this you will need to create a lead magnet and offer your audience something which is incredibly valuable to them for free. There are numerous ways you can do this and which one you use will depend very much on what type of business you are and what your goals are. If you are a business offering technical solutions then you could offer them a free trial, if you are offering information then you could offer them a free report, a short video training series or an ebook. If you are selling some kind of product or service you could offer them a money off voucher, these work particularly well for restaurants and the service industry as a whole. Whatever you are offering, it needs to be really good to attract your audience and get them to volunteer their email.

Here are the features you need to have on your website or blog or any landing page with a special offer.

- **Keep your design simple** Your site needs to have a clean and simple design and you need to communicate your most important message clearly and concisely to your target audience. Your most important content with any call to action needs to be placed above the fold, where they will be easily seen and your call to action should have an easily seen button link rather than just a text link.

- **Make your site easy to navigate** Really this is so important, try to use the minimum number of pages you can and make your menu titles as easy to understand.

- **Clearly communicate your message** You want your visitors to subscribe to your opt-in so you need to place your compelling offer with an image and title of the offer somewhere where it is visible. The message and benefit of your offer needs be descriptive and specific.

- **Add a clear call to action** In order for your visitors to sign up they will need to be told what to do. Make sure you have a direct call to action, for example, 'Download your free ebook now' or 'Sign up for your discount voucher now.' Your call to action needs to be clearly visible with an eye catching button link which is much more effective than a text link.

- **Add clear contact information** Make it easy for your prospects to contact you by placing your contact details where they will be easily seen. With the technology available you can even add chat features so that as soon as your prospect arrives on your site a chat form appears asking if you can be of any assistance. Obviously you need the resources to be able to man this but it is an incredibly powerful way of quickly building trust and showing how much you value your website visitors by being available to answer any of their questions.

- **Email capture form** Your email capture form needs to be as simple as possible, preferably just asking for their name and email. You need to state on the form that their email address is safe with you and will not be shared with anyone. Make sure your form is in a prominent position and consider using a pop-up form that appears after 20 seconds after your prospect has arrived on your site. Your email sign up form needs to go at the top, the side and the bottom of your webpage and also on your 'about page' which is often the most popular page on your site.

- **Privacy policy** You need a clear privacy policy on your website and to make it clear that you will not be spamming them or selling their information.

- **Thank you page** Once your visitor has completed the form you will have them as a lead, but before you let them go you can send them to a thank you page where you can offer them the opportunity to share your offer with their friends by including social sharing buttons.

- **Mobile Friendly** You need to make sure your offer is easily visible and easy to complete on mobile. This is incredibly important as more and more people are purchasing from their mobiles and there is nothing more annoying for the user if the site is hard to navigate from their mobile.

- Don't add external links to other sites. Be careful not to fall into the trap of wanting to make your site more interesting by adding lots of content and links to other external sites as this will only detract from your main goals and you'll end up sending traffic away from your site.

Landing pages

Landing pages are incredibly effective if you want to promote specific offers for specific products to specific audiences. A landing page is a page that is designed to give information about an offer and then capture a lead with a form for your visitor to complete so that the visitor can download or claim that offer. Landing pages are highly effective in capturing leads because they are designed to be specific in their goal, which is to capture the contact information of your visitor.

The landing page should have a clear uncluttered design and not have any links or navigation menus that could take your visitor away from the landing page and it should contain the following:

- A headline. (The title of the offer)
- A description of the offer clearly detailing the benefits to your visitor.

- A compelling image of the offer.
- A clear call to action. This can be in the form of an image or text.
- A form to capture contact information. (The fewer fields that are required to be completed the more leads you will receive)
- A clear privacy policy on your website that makes it clear that you will not be spamming them or selling their information.
- A thank you page leading them to another offer or social sharing.

You can either ask your web developer to create landing pages or there are numerous tools available on the internet where you can easily create one, for example: www.leadpages.net www.unbounce.com www.launcheffect.com and www.instapage.com

SETTING UP YOUR EMAIL CAMPAIGN

Once you have created your lead capture system on your website, blog, or separate landing page and have your subscribers permission to send them your email you are going to need a really good email campaign to convert those leads into sales.

Email is still one of the most effective forms of converting leads into sales and email is more powerful than ever. Not only is it cost effective but it also provides one of the most direct and personal lines of communication with your customer. Once subscribed they have invited you into their inbox on a regular basis and producing valuable content for your subscribers will develop trust and deepen your relationship with your subscribers. Your email will also work hand in hand with your YouTube campaign. As you build your relationship with your subscribers on YouTube, they are more likely to deem your emails valuable and open them.

The first thing you need to do is set yourself up with a good email marketing provider and there are many you can choose from: www.aweber.com www.constantcontact.com www.mailchimp.com to name a few. It's important to use a system where you have a confirmed opt-in, this is when the subscriber is sent an email to confirm their email address. This confirms that you are gaining consent and legally protects you, it also helps you to keep a clean list and it protects you from sending email to incorrect addresses. You can then automate your emails with an auto responder and send out emails automatically over time.

Your next task is to plan and create your email campaign. Here are a few tips for doing so:

- **Be clear about your goals** You need to be absolutely clear from day one what you want to achieve through email. Are you using it to introduce a new product at some time? Are you launching an event? Whatever you do make sure you know exactly what it is that you want to achieve.

- **Keep it simple and in line with your branding** Make sure your email design ties in with your branding. Most email providers offer templates which you can add your own branding to, or you can get a designer to create a particular design. Keep it really simple, sometimes if things are too fancy they become impersonal.

- **Send a regular newsletter** Plan to send a regular newsletter email at least once a month and once a week if you can. You can also plan to send one off information about offers which tie in with special holidays and occasions throughout the year, or competitions or events that you may be planning.

- **Plan your topics** You need to plan the topics you want to cover in each email and this should tie in nicely with the plan for your blog articles. You then need to deliver high quality content which is tailor made to fit with your subscribers interests and it needs to be so good that they are looking forward to the next email from you. If you are sending emails about offers then you need to show them clearly how these offers are going to benefit their lives.

- **Attention grabbing titles** This is where you need to get really creative. Your main goal here is to get your subscriber to open your email and you need to create a headline that is going to make your subscriber curious and inquisitive and eager to open your mail. Questions work really well as titles and you will often see your open rates increase. This is because people find questions intriguing and they feel like you are directly addressing them. Try and avoid the words that will trigger spam filters, simply search Google for a list of these words to avoid.

- **Be authentic and true to your brand** Write your emails in a style that your audience will grow to recognise, like and identify with your brand. Write so your subscriber feels like you are just writing to them. You need to establish yourself as a likeable expert for your subscribers. Try and create a personal relationship with them by addressing them by name and giving them a warm friendly introduction. Offering them the opportunity to connect with you and answer any of their questions by simply replying to the mail is a great way to build trust.

- **Keep it simple** Make sure your emails are simply constructed and straight to the point so you keep your subscribers interest and get them quickly to the place you want them to go, like your blog, or your offer.

- **Include social sharing buttons** Include all your social sharing icons and links in your mail.

- **Make them feel safe** Make sure your subscribers are clear that their email will not be shared, that they can unsubscribe anytime.

- **Analyse your open rates** Most email service providers include statistics in their packages so you can analyse open rates, bounce rates, click through rates, unsubscribers and social sharing statistics. These results give you the opportunity to find out what is and what is not working.

CHAPTER ELEVEN

BLOG BLOG BLOG

THIS CHAPTER IS for anyone who does not have a blog. The word blog has been mentioned numerous times throughout the book and has become an essential part of any online business today.

WHAT IS A BLOG?

A blog (short for web log) is a term used to describe a website that provides an ongoing journal of individual news stories which are based around a certain subject or subjects (blog posts). Blogs have given people the power of the media. Anyone can now create a personal type of news that appeals to a high number of small niche audiences.

Bloggers simply complete a simple online form with a title and body and then post it. The Blog post then appears at the top of the website as the most recent article. Over time the posts build up to become a collection of posts which are then archived chronologically for easy reference. Each blog post can then become a discussion with space for comments below the post, readers can leave comments and questions. This is where bloggers start to build relationships and a community with their readers and other bloggers who may have similar interests. Blogs were one of the earliest forms of social media and started growing in the late 1990s. The number of blogs has exploded in recent years and blogs now underpin the majority of successful social media campaigns.

WHY BLOG FOR BUSINESS?

Blogging is one of the most beneficial tools that a business has to get found online, to communicate knowledge and expertise and engage with prospects and customers. Businesses can share information about their business and about any subject that may be of interest to their niche. It is a fact that businesses with blogs benefit from an increase in the number of visitors to their website, increased leads, increase in inbound links and increased sales. Here are some of the reasons why and the benefits that come with blogging:

- **Underpins your whole social media campaign** Your blog is the focus of all your social media efforts and the centre of all your content marketing efforts. One of the main goals of any business today will be to get people to their blog to read their valuable and targeted content and social media will be one of the main tools they can use to drive traffic to their blog.

- **Increased Website traffic** A well optimised blog will increase your chances of being found in search. Google loves unique fresh content and if this is created regularly, this will boost your traffic.

- Builds brand awareness A Blog offers a business the opportunity to build a community and build awareness for their products or services. The more people who see your blog, the more people see your brand.

- **Provides valuable information for your niche** Creating a Blog gives your business a voice and provides your niche with valuable information in relation to the subjects that they are interested in. This may include information about market trends, industry news and insight into your products and services and what is behind them.

- **Thought leadership** Sharing your expertise with valuable information will make you stand out as a thought leader in your particular field and will help you to build a professional online reputation.

- **Builds Trust & creates warm leads** When you are providing valuable content for your niche on a regular basis, answering their questions and addressing their concerns, this in turn creates trust between you and your prospective customers. This trust leads to more leads and will result in sales. When your audience become regular readers of your blog they become warm rather than cold leads, the ice has been broken and they are half way there in terms of buying your product.

- You gain more and more knowledge While writing your blog you will be continually researching your subject, learning about new technology, products and new trends. In turn, this keeps you ahead of the game and in the eyes of your customers it makes you an expert. As time goes by you become more and more knowledgable and can steer your business in line with market trends and keep your products and services up to the minute. You will also find that blogging is inspiring and your ideas will snowball, as you learn more material you will find more material to blog about.

- **Interaction and Feedback** When your blog has room for comments and discussion it will give you the opportunity to hear what people are saying, the questions they are asking and insight into what they want out of your products. Feedback like this is invaluable to your business and also leads to more ideas for more blog posts. This kind of feedback also encourages a conversation and you actually get the opportunity to communicate with prospective customers.

HOW TO CREATE A BLOG

Creating your blog is incredibly straight forward. There are a number of free blogging platforms that are available, however, if you read the terms and conditions of most of these platforms you will find that at the end of the day you do not actually own the content and you will not have full control of your blog. You will have no control of the advertising displayed, you are unlikely to be able to include an email capture form, you will not be able to have you own domain name and you will not be able to install plugins. With a free platform your domain name will look something like http://mybusinessblog.theirblogplatformname.com and overall it is not going to look that professional.

The best and safest way of creating a blog and running with your own domain name is to create one with wordpress.org which will give you full control over your site. Wordpress.org is a free open source platform which means it can be modified and customised and by anyone. You can use custom themes or you can choose from hundreds of free themes and plugins. The wordpress.org blogging platform is free but you will need to purchase a domain name and host your site on your own server, however most hosting companies offer inexpensive monthly plans and a one click installation solutions. You will also need to make sure you back up your blog and you may very well find this is included in your hosting package.

WHAT MAKES A SUCCESSFUL BLOG

For those businesses that are doing it right blogging can be hugely beneficial and they will often see an increase of over 50% of website visitors and leads. However, many blogs also fail to make any positive difference to a business, so it is essential that before you waste time and resources you understand what you need to do to create a successful blog:.

Set Goals and objectives

First of all you will need to be about clear what your marketing goals are and set clear objectives for what you want to achieve from your blog.

Example Goal 1

To support YouTube Channel with blog.

Objective:
To post video on Blog and create a blog post around the subject.

Example Goal 2
Increase brand awareness through blog.
Objective:
Achieve X number of shares per month on social media.

Example Goal 3
Increase Traffic to website from blog.
Objective: To achieve an increase of X Traffic from blog.

Example Goal 4
Increase the number of leads for product A.
Objective: To gain X number of new opt-ins per week.

Example Goal 5
To create interaction and engagement.
Objective: To have at least X number of comments on each blog post.

Example Goal 6
To become a thought leader in the industry.
Objective: To write X number of guest posts per month/year.

Example Goal 7
To increase the ranking of blog in Google and Bing.
Objective: To achieve X number of backlinks from other websites in 6 months.

Create top content for your audience
Again it's all about your audience and what they want, what they are interested in, what makes them tick and what problems they need solving. If you can identify these things then you are half way to finding the

valuable content that is going to keep your audience interested and engaged. When you create your content it needs to be either inspiring, educational, informative or entertaining. If you can create content that people really value, they are more likely to share your content, more likely to sign up for your updates and more likely to come back looking for more. Creating content around your product or services is not going to provide enough interest to your readers and it is unlikely to get shared. Of course the occasional post is ok but try and keep away from this unless you can tie it in with something which is of real value to your audience.

Create a content plan

Your content plan is the backbone to your blog. You will need to decide what topics you are going to build your blog around so that you can stay consistent. There may be certain keywords that you want to target and need to incorporate into your content. Once you know your topics or subjects then you can decide which types of posts you are going to create. There are numerous types of blog posts you can use, for example; tutorials, how to's , interviews, reviews, book reviews, advice, Q and A's, case studies, trend reports and the latest news in your industry. When you have decided on all this you then write a schedule and if you have certain events that happen every year in your industry make sure you include these in your plan.

Newsworthy posts

Make sure you are blogging about whats new in your industry and keep an eye on trending topics relating to your industry so you can create blog posts that are really up to date. You can do this by checking out what is trending on the social sites and also signing up for Google alerts which will keep you up to date on new info relating to your interests and queries.

Frequent and consistent blogging

It is proven that the more high quality content you produce, the more views your blog will get. You will need to post at least once a week if not more. Google loves fresh content so the more posts you have, the more opportunities you are going to have to be found.

Optimise your blog for search

Look for keywords and phrases that people are looking for. There are tools available to do this like word tracker, Google trends and Google keyword planner. You can find out the amount of competition by typing a phrase into Google search and seeing how many results it brings up. In order to get found you will need to concentrate your efforts on low competition keywords and phrases and the more specific your words and phrases are the better. You can then create your content around your chosen keyword or phrase as long as the content is highly relevant. When creating your blog post make sure you put the word/phrase in the page title, the header and the body. If you put the phrase in your meta tag it will be displayed in bold font in the search results which will make it stand out even more.

Attention grabbing headline

To catch your readers attention you need a good headline, a headline that will need to intrigue your audience enough to make them feel that they absolutely have to read this post. It needs to be simple and to the point as well as containing valuable keywords. Here are some example headlines that really work:

How to ....

7 ways to successfully ....

Why you should do ..... to ....

Secrets that every ...... should know.

The secret formula for success in ......

5 quick and easy ways to ....

What every serious ...... should know about......

7 things every ..... should avoid to ......

A great design

Your blog needs to be inviting and although the content is what people are looking for the blog still needs to be visually appealing and reflect your brand. If your blog is just text based it's going to look cold and uninviting and lack interest, so you need to include compelling images to engage your audience. It is definitely a good idea to spend time researching different themes. Another thing to watch with your design is your side bar, make sure you have only what is absolutely necessary so you do not pull your readers attention away from the action you want them to take.

Formatting

You need to make it as easy as possible for your reader to read and digest your blog. If you format your blog with headings, bold subtitles and bullet points it will be a much more enjoyable to read than one long paragraph.

Ask a question at the end of your post

Asking a question at the end of your post is likely to provoke discussion. People like to think their opinions matter and it's a great way for your readers to interact and network with each other too. Make sure you answer any questions your readers ask, there is nothing worse than seeing bloggers ignoring their readers.

Tags

Tags help people to find your content within your blog and with the search engines, they also help to group related posts together.

11 *THINGS EVERY BLOG SHOULD HAVE*

An incentive to join your opt-in

One of the main goals of your blog is to captures leads. The majority of your readers will probably only read one of your blog posts so it's really important to try and get them on your opt-in list so they will keep reading your blog. You will need to make sure you give them some kind of incentive to complete the email capture form like a free report, free ebook, or simply email updates.

An engaging image

A blog needs at least one image to make it look interesting and inviting. Blogs without images are simply boring. You can use your own images, stock photos or use images from photo sharing sites like Flickr.

Clear call to actions

You need to make it very clear both within your text and outside your text what you want your readers to do. This could be anything from signing up for email update, a free trial, a free offer, a request for a quote or more information on a product.

Email capture form

You can either including a prominent form on your blog, or by installing a pop up mail capture form. If you do install a pop up then make sure the reader has a good few seconds to read the heading and start reading the article before the form pops up. It is also a good practice to put at least three email sign up forms on the page, one below the article, one in the footer and one on the top beside the article or right above it.

About section

Your about section is the introduction to you and your blog. It's probably the most viewed page of any blog. People like to know who is writing the blog and feel acquainted with that person, so you need to get your personality over in this section. Make sure you include your name and a picture of yourself, this will help your readers make a personal connection with you. A video of yourself is also a great a way of getting your readers acquainted too. Above all focus on how you are going to help your readers, what problems you are going to solve for them and introduce some of the topics you are going to talk about. Remember your blog is about your audience's needs and not yours.

Contact page

A simple contact form works best but also make it really easy for people to reach out to you. Make sure you include all your social sharing buttons and an email capture form.

Easy to search archives

If the content of your blog posts are interesting then your readers are going to want to read more so you need to make the previous blog posts easily accessible. On many sites it really is incredibly difficult to find content, so you will need to get yourself a custom archive page, and a search box at the top of your blog is a great idea for helping your readers to find content.

Social sharing plugins

You need to include buttons or links to all the social networks where you have a presence. There are hundreds of plugins you can use to do this. Also make sure you have sharing buttons next to your articles as well.

RSS Feed

RSS (Rich Site Summary) is a format for delivering regularly changing content on the internet. It saves you from checking the sites you are interested in for new content. Instead it retrieves the content from sites you are interested in. Make sure you have the RSS feed and then have a clear call to action making it clear why they should subscribe to your feed. If you want to keep up to date with your favourite bloggers you can sign up to either My Yahoo, www.bloglines.com or www.newsgator.com

Comments section

Your blog needs a comment section which will encourage interaction and help you to build relationships with your readers. You can install Facebook comments easily with a Wordpress plugin or Disqus is another favourite comment provider.

A guest bloggers welcome page

Guest posting is becoming more and more important in the blogging community and making it obvious that you will accept guest posts is going to go a long way to building relationships with other bloggers. The benefits of having other people contributing to your blog are that you will have more valuable content on your site and more exposure if your guest blogger promotes their posts on their site. You may also gain from the opportunity to produce a guest post on their blog at a later date. Guest blogging is a top method of getting back links to your blog which is essential for search engine optimisation.

Privacy policy & terms of service pages

Make it clear your email readers are safe with you and you are not going to share their information with any other parties.

PROMOTING YOUR BLOG

If you want to run a successful blog then you cannot just rely on search to get it out into the blogosphere, you need to find other ways of promoting your content and getting found.

- **Promote on your social sites** Posting your blog content on social sites is essential. You can connect your blog to Twitter and Facebook so your content is automatically shared. Or you can use Hootsuite or Tweetdec to share your content to multiple sites which will save you time. When posting use an image to grab your audience's attention and make sure you use popular hashtags for your topic which will open up more opportunities to being found by new people.

- **Guest blogging** Guest blogging is a great way of gaining a larger following. It will also give your blog more exposure, credibility and increase your inbound links which is essential for SEO. Most bloggers allow guest bloggers to post their bio including their social profiles and blog URL on their site.

- **Social sharing buttons** As mentioned previously it is essential to have social sharing buttons next to your blog articles.

- **Comment on other blogs** There is so much opportunity for you to promote yourself today with the number of blogs and social sites. If you comment on other peoples blogs you can often leave a URL but only if it is relevant to the article being commented on and you are adding some value to the article.

- **Website and email** If you have a website then try and point people to your blog. You can do this by adding visual links on your about page and other pages. Also make sure you have a link to your blog in your email and send an email to your current contacts telling them about your blog.

- **Create a Google Adwords campaign** If you are serious about driving traffic to your site and generating leads and you have your blog set up to catch leads and subscribers then an Adwords campaign may kick start your traffic while you are waiting for your blog to get found naturally in search results. Getting quick results like this will also allow you to see if your blog design and format is working and whether any incentives you are offering are enough to generate subscribers and leads.

- **Submit your blog to Reddit and Stumbleupon** Both of these websites allow their uses to rate web content. Reddit is a collection of webpages which have been submitted by its users. Stumbleupon is a collection of web pages that have been given the thumbs up. You can submit pages directly on its submit page or by installing the firefox add-on, or the chrome extension. It is best not add too many of your own pages to Stumbleupon but make sure you add both the Reddit and the Stumbleupon buttons to your blog so other people can.

THE ESSENTIAL WORDPRESS PLUGINS

One of the best things about Wordpress for your blog is that it is easy to customise and you need little or no technical or design knowledge to create a great blog. There are a ton of plugins you can install to make your site even better but there are so many it is difficult to choose which ones are really important. To help you here are some plugins that are essential for your blog:

- **The Facebook comments plugin** Installing Facebook comments into your blog can be tricky but with this easy to use plugin you can easily administer and customise Facebook comments from your Wordpress site. Another plugin, **Facebook comments SEO** will insert a Facebook comment form, Open Graph Tags, and insert all Facebook comments into your Wordpress database for better search engine optimisation. When it comes to spammers, Facebook with Open Graph is managing to weed out spammers and trolls with great effectiveness. Facebook allows you to login with Facebook, Yahoo and Microsoft Live.

- **Disqus Comment System** The other popular comment system Disqus replaces your wordpress comment system with comments hosted and powered by Disqus. It features threaded comments and replies, notifications and replies by email, aggregated comments and social mentions and full spam filtering, black and white lists. Disqus allows you to login with Facebook, Twitter and Google.

- **Facebook Chat.** This is great if you want to chat with your visitors in real time. When installed Facebook Chat will display on the bottom right. This is great for supplying support on your site.

- **Broken Link Checker** This essential plugin scans your site and notifies you if it finds any broken links or missing images and then lets you replace the link with one that works.

- **RB Internal Links** This plugin assists you with internal links and cuts the risk of error pages and broken links.

- **Social Sharing Plugins** There are numerous social sharing plugins available for wordpress. **Flare** is a simple yet eye-catching sharing bar that you can customise depending on which buttons you want to display. It helps to get you followed or liked and helps get your content shared via posts, pages and media types. The other great feature Flare has is that you can display your Flare at the top, bottom or right of your post content. When Flare is displayed on the left and right of your posts it follows your visitors down the page and conveniently hides when not needed. Other social sharing plugins include: **Floating Social Media Icon, Social Stickers** and **Shareaholic** to name but a few.

- **All In One Schema Rich Snippets** Rich Snippets are markup tags that webmasters can put in their sites in order to tell Google what type of content they have on their site so that Google can better display it in search results, it is basically a short summary of your page. Rich snippets are very interactive and let you stand out from your competition and help with your search engine ranking. Unless you are a techie then implementing them can be tricky however this plugin makes it really simple by giving you a meta box to fill in every time you create a new blog post.

- **Contact Form Plugins** It is very important to make it easy for your visitors to contact you and a form really does help with this. There are numerous plugins available for you to easily install and here are a few: **Contact 7, Fast Secure Contact form, Contact form and Contactme.**

- **Simple Pull Quote** The Simple Pull Quote Wordpress plugin provides an easy way for you to insert and pull quotes into your blog posts. This is great for bringing attention to important pieces of information and adding interest to a post.

- **Backup Plugins** Backing up your Files and database is essential. It maybe that your hosting service provides this but there are very good plugins that do this: Vaultpress, BackWPup, Backup buddy and Backup.

- **Related Posts Plugins** Related post plugins help your visitors to stay on your site by analysing the content on your site and pulling in similar articles from your site for them to read. One of the most popular ones is **nrelate related** content which is simple to install and activate. **Wordpress related posts** is another one.

- **Search Everything Plugin** This plugin increases the ability of the Wordpress search and you can configure it to search for anything you choose.

- **Google Analytics Plugin** The Google Analytics plugin allows you to easily integrate Google Analytics using Google Analytics tracking code.

- **Google XML Sitemaps** It is essential that the search engines can index your site and this plugin will generate a special XML sitemap.

- **SEO Friendly images** This plugin automatically adds alt and title attributes to all your images which helps to improve traffic from search engines.

- **Akismet (Comments and Spam)** The more traffic you receive the more likely it is for you to receive spam and fake comments. Akismet checks your comments against Akismet web services to see if they look like spam or not and then lets you review it under your comments admin screen.

- **Social Author Bio** Social author Bio automatically adds an author box along with Gravatar and social icons on posts.

- **Yoast** Yoast is a free SEO wordpress plugin which helps to optimise your site's titles and descriptions.

- **Thank Me Later** This great little plugin automatically sends a thank you note by email to anyone who has commented on your blog. You can personalise your email and set up exactly when you want to send it and you can set it up to only send it out once, or set it up as a chain of emails. This plugin is great for engaging people who comment on your blog and you could use it to encourage people to join your opt-in.

MEASURING YOUR RESULTS

Measuring the success of your blog is crucial in order to steer your blog in the right direction so that your business can benefit from all the rewards a top blog can offer. Here are a number of ways you can measure your success:

Google Analytics

You can easily measure the number of social media shares, number of leads, subscribers and comments on your blog. For more detailed information on your blog performance then setting up a Google Analytics account is essential and will offer you a wealth of detailed information so you can measure results including the following:

- **The number of back links** In the left side bar under **Standard Reports** you will find a section **Traffic Sources** and then under **Social** you will find **Trackbacks**. You will find here any web pages that have linked to any page of your site with the number of visits.

- **The number of visits** Obviously this is one of the most important statistics and you will be able to see easily how many visits you have and information about where your traffic is coming from.

- **Page Views** You will be able to see which pages are generating the most interest and therefore you will be able to plan more content similar to this.

- **Keywords** You can keep track of your success with how your traffic is being generated by keywords. You will be able to see if your optimisation for certain keywords is working and whether your blog is being found by keywords that you had not considered. When you identify which keywords are the most popular you can try and work them into other blog posts.

- **Conversions** In Google Analytics you will also be able to track conversions which is an action on your site which is important to your business. This could be a download, sign up or purchase. You will need to define your goals in analytics in order to track the conversion. You will be able to see conversion rates and also the value of conversions if you set a monetary value. There are detailed instructions available in Google Analytics on how to set this up or you can employ web developer or specialist to set this up.

Chapter Twelve

The Icing on The Cake

FOLLOWING ALL THE steps, instructions and strategies is going to go a long way to making your campaign succeed, but what does it take to make you really good? If you have ever followed or are following certain brands on social media you will probably have discovered that there are certain brands or businesses that stand out from the crowd. These are the brands and businesses that seem bigger than their products. These are the ones who usually have a sizeable and highly targeted audience, the best quality content, the greatest amount of interaction and engagement and they often post viral content. They literally have their audience hanging on their every word and get the highest open rates for their emails. They appear to understand their audience and relate to them by going out of their way by either helping them to achieve their dreams, calm their fears or confirm their suspicions and offer them incredible value. It is obvious by the interaction that they have built a loving and respecting community and you can be almost sure that all this is transferring to their balance sheets. These businesses are what I call, 'The Social Media Superstars' they are the game changers and they truly know how to leverage the power of social media to work for their business.

These 'Social Media Superstars' can often be compared to those party animals, the ones who always seem to be the most popular at any party and are more often than not surrounded by an audience of engaged and happy people having a great time. These people also always seem to be the most interesting, the most interested, the most charismatic, the most engaged, and they almost always tend to be good listeners as well. So how can you emulate this scenario and what does it take to stand out from the crowd in YouTube marketing?

It's all about your audience and a few other things!
The reasons these individuals, businesses and brands are good at social media marketing is not because they have particular powers, it's not by chance or by coincidence, it's because they know that it's all about the audience and a few other things!

Of course your aim is to ultimately benefit your business but in order to do this you need to make it all about your audience and what they want. If you give them what they want by either making their life better or easier in some way or solving a problem they may have, then you are going to build a valuable base of subscribers who trust you, open your emails and who are ready to go to the next step and buy your product. You will find that your subscribers will become ambassadors and advocates and will then be doing the work for you by sharing your content and promoting your brand in the most powerful way, word of mouth. To achieve this and stand out from the crowd you need to go the extra mile by doing the following:

- Being fully committed and positive about your campaign and in it for the long term.
- Totally believing in what you are offering,This could be your product, your service or yourself if you are a personal brand.
- Making it all about your audience, knowing exactly who they are, what makes them tick, what they need and how to connect with them.
- Putting your audience's needs above your own and demonstrating the rich content and service you provide.
- Putting the relationship with your audience first, by listening to them, understanding them and embracing conversation where you can.
- Offering your audience incredible value with free information and advice.

- Being authentic and true to your brand.

So if there is one piece of insight I want to leave you with it is this:

IT'S ALL ABOUT YOUR AUDIENCE and WHAT THEY WANT
I really hope you have enjoyed the book, that you have found it of great value and you will continue using it as your manual for your success on YouTube. The world of Social Media is continually changing and it is my commitment to keep updating the books as and when these changes happen. If you would like to continue receiving these social media updates by email please sign up at www.alexstearn.com

I would love your feedback about the book and would be very grateful if you could take just a moment to leave a review on Amazon and of course please feel fee to contact me if you have any questions at alex@alexstearn.com

Lastly, I have also written a series covering all the major social media platforms including: Twitter, Google + , LinkedIn™, Pinterest, Instagram, Tumblr, YouTube and the big one, Make Social Media work for your Business. All are available on Amazon and Kindle. I will also be continually posting helpful and inspirational tips, building a community on YouTube and look forward to connecting with you there or on any of your preferred social networks.

Website: www.alexstearn.com
www.facebook.com/alexandrastearn
www.instagram.com/alexstearn
www.twitter.com/alexstearncom
www.pinterest.com/alexstearn
www.alexstearn.tumblr.com
www.youtube.com/alexstearn

www.linkedin.com/in/alexstearn
www.google.com/+alexstearn

Other Books in the Series

Make Social Media Work For Your Business

Make Facebook Work For Your Business

Make Twitter Work For Your Business

Make Instagram Work For Your Business

Make Pinterest Work For Your Business

Make Google + Work For Your Business

Make Tumblr Work For Your Business

Printed in Great Britain
by Amazon.co.uk, Ltd.,
Marston Gate.